"Its business is . . . simply to know the best that is known and thought in the world, and by in its turn making that known to create a current of true and fresh ideas."

Arnold, *Functions of Criticism At The Present Time*, 1865.

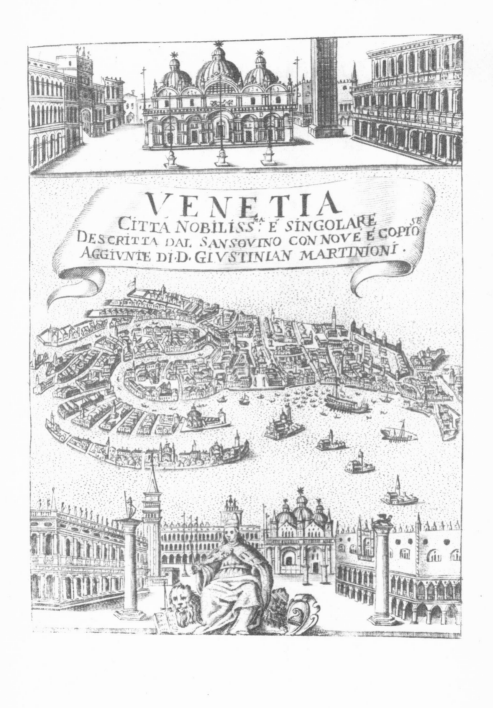

VENETIA

CITTÀ NOBILISS.MA E SINGOLARE
DESCRITTA DAL SANSOVINO CON NOVE E COPIOSE
AGGIVNTE DI D. GIVSTINIAN MARTINIONI.

Venice Recorded

A GUIDE BOOK AND ANTHOLOGY
WRITTEN AND COMPILED BY

Milton Grundy

ANGUS & ROBERTSON (U.K.) LTD
2 FISHER STREET
LONDON, W.C.1

Acknowledgments

The author and publisher wish to thank the following publishers and individuals who have kindly granted permission to quote throughout this anthology, and to illustrate the walks:

George Allen and Unwin, Ltd., *Venice* by A. J. Hare; *Modern Painters* and *The Stones of Venice* by John Ruskin: The Athlone Press, *A History of Architecture on the Comparative Method* by Banister Fletcher: Clarendon Press, Oxford, *The Italian Painters of the Renaissance* by Bernard Berenson: Collins, *The Italian Journey* by J. W. Goethe, translated by W. H. Auden and Elizabeth Mayer; *Companion Guide to Venice* by Hugh Honour: Elek Books, Limited, *Venice: The Masque of Italy* by Marcel Brion: The Financial Times, *Canute-like by the Sea* by Peter Tumiati: Instituto Poligraphica dello Stato, *Venice and Its Lagoons* by Giulio Lorenzetti: Macdonald & Co. (Publishers) Ltd., *Italian Food* by Elizabeth David: Methuen & Co. Ltd., *Permanent Red* by John Berger; *A Wanderer in Venice* by E. V. Lucas: l'Oeil, published by Georges Bernier, *Venice Observed: Notes on the Plates* by Andre Chastel: Max Parrish, *The Lagoons of Venice* by Sylvia Sprigge: Penguin Books, Ltd., *An Outline of European Architecture* by Nicolas Pevsner; *Art and Architecture of Italy* by Rudolf Wittkower: Phaidon Press, Ltd.. *Civilization of the Renaissance in Italy* by J. Burckhart; *The Story of Art* by E. H. Gombrich; *An Introduction to Italian Renaissance Painting* by Cecil Gould; *Painting in Eighteenth Century Venice* by Michael Levey: Princeton University Press, *A Renascence of Early Christian Art in Thirteenth Century Venice* by Otto Demus: Edition d'Art Albert Skira, *The Venice of Carpaccio* by T. Pignatti: Thames and Hudson, Ltd., *The Renaissance in Italy* by H. Decker; *Italian Villas and Palaces* by Georgina Masson.

For most of the pictures in the book by courtesy of the trustees of the British Museum, Prints and Drawings Department, and photographed by John R. Freeman, Ltd.

and
Reproduced by gracious permission of Her Majesty Queen Elizabeth II, from the Royal Library, Windsor Castle: pages 177, 191

The Giorgio Cini Foundation: pages 107 and 204
The Correr Museum: page 56 (top)
The Goethe-Schiller Archives, Weimar: page 76

Front Endpapers: Venice in 1500 by Jacopo de' Barbari
Frontispiece: Venetia, a title page of a guide to Venice published in 1663

Maps by Jan van der Watering

Contents

Illustrations

Venice in A.D. 421, as envisaged by an eighteenth-century artist.

Preface

Writing a guide-book is an act of love. The desire to share with others what we ourselves have enjoyed, have excitedly discovered or re-discovered through frequent visits, at times enriched by comparing our impressions with those of other visitors of years—or even centuries —gone by.

As can be the case in Venice, a city observed, admired or detested, which has never left travellers indifferent. After the catastrophic 'high water' of November 4th, 1966, the British 'Italian Art and Archives Rescue Fund' was among the very first to *rush* to the rescue of Venice, fully realising that the dramatic disaster of Florence had its subtler and more lethal counterpart in our city's floods. It was in fact that flooding of 1966 (we might almost be glad to consider it a blessing in disguise had it not caused such incalculable damage) which at last focussed the eyes of the world upon this unique city and its plight. UNESCO, the cultural arm of the United Nations, was drawn into the battle for the preservation of Venice. Other national committees from the United States, France, Germany, Holland, brought aid to Venice after having worked wonders in Florence. The Italian government gave generously, and the great 'operation salvation' was on. Today UNESCO is collaborating on all fronts. Many new committees have come into being—to replace those which had been formed after the disaster of 1966 and were of a temporary nature—and we have an Italian committee which is restoring the church of Santo Stefano, the Scuola di San Giorgio degli Schiavoni where the famous Carpacios hang, and the great Palladian church of the Redentore.

The perfect example of what can be accomplished by such organisa-tions is the Church of La Madonna dell'Orto, which now stands totally restored and newly brought to life thanks to the 'Italian Art and Archives Rescue Fund' in collaboration with the Italian government.

The 'Venice in Peril Fund' is now taking over as a permanent British Committee for Venice where the temporary one stopped. There is a long story behind this love-affair between the Queen of the Adriatic and her imperial successor as ruler of the seas. These merchant-queens must surely have something in common that binds them, island-status both, defended and isolated by the sea, who draw their strength and power from the encircling waters.

And now that Venice has lost all, now that she lies prostrate under the attacks of that very element which once enriched her—and under the even more dangerous attacks of a new race of men so far removed from those who created and worshipped her—who should guide her British friends through the intricacies of 'calli' and canals but an English cicerone who illustrates the beauties of the ailing 'queen' by using not only his own expressions of admiration or criticism but also those of a great chorus of voices—some of today, others that come back to us from the distant past?

The cicerone, Milton Grundy, has generously offered to devolve his author's royalties for this excellent publication to the Italian Committee for Venice. One more proof of true attachment to our city.

Venice has never been as greatly in need of love as she is today. She can and must be preserved. But this will happen only if an ever-growing chorus of voices will be raised once more, but this time not so much to sing her praises as to demand her preservation. To explain why we cannot afford to lose her, why our whole spiritual world would be so much the poorer were Venice to disappear. Thanks to the Author's admirable presentation of our Treasures many new allies will surely be gained to our cause. And his gift to us will encourage the Italian Committee for Venice to keep on fighting a battle which has the support of such friends as Mr. Grundy.

Anna Maria Cicogna Volpi

Introduction

This book is essentially an anthology arranged as a guide book. It is a common experience that the information provided for the tourist (both in books and by human guides) falls miserably short of the best that has been thought and said on the subject. In Venice I find this particularly galling, for it is a significant part of the experience of the place that other and far more distinguished visitors have been before and pondered upon the very sight that is before one's eyes. I have therefore chosen what seem to me to be the most illuminating passages from their writings, and arranged these in the context of tours of the town. Something of this kind was done by Augustus Hare at the turn of the century. But I have looked in vain for a modern equivalent, and (not for the first time in my life) I find I have had to write the book I wanted to read. In doing this I have had to make a number of basic decisions, and perhaps at this stage I should say what they are.

In the first place, I have concentrated on passages which illuminate particular pictures, buildings or views. I have omitted passages which throw light only on their author (though with Ruskin I have made some exceptions, for he is such a towering phenomenon that I expect the reader may be interested in him in his own right).

You will notice, too, that I do not expect the reader to see everything. If you are in Venice for three months you will be able to make use of *Venice* by Giulio Lorenzetti—a thorough and scholarly work (to which I have referred ceaselessly in preparing this book). In a stay of two weeks (or in the first two weeks of a longer stay) it is plainly better to take an informed look at a relatively small number of masterpieces, than to tramp in an uninformed way past a bewildering number of objects of diverse styles, periods and quality. I have therefore had to make a lot of decisions about what to include and what to omit. I have not found it necessary to depart in any radical way from currently accepted notions of what are masterpieces, but I have made a conscious effort not to be influenced by famous names, and I have not hesitated to omit things which do not live up to their reputations. I have also

11

(though with some reluctance) left out a few things simply on the grounds that they are too far away from the seven areas into which I have divided the town, but none of these is of major importance.

The city calls for a variety of responses—the earnestness of Ruskin can be felt as inappropriate at some times, as can the 'amused' stance of James Morris at others. The one response which—as the reader will inevitably discover for himself—is unproductive at all times is art-indigestion, and I should perhaps stress—especially for the more serious minded visitor—that there is such a thing as an experience of the town as a whole, which is not obtained by scurrying (with however refined and informed a sensibility) from one picture or building to another. You will see that I propose only seven principal excursions: I suggest that not every morning be devoted to sightseeing, but that a lot of one's time in Venice ought to be devoted to doing nothing in particular —strolling in the Piazza, taking morning coffee in some *campo*, or just getting lost in the maze of small alleyways.

The pundits insist that the only way to approach Venice is from the sea. No doubt they are right; the visitor from Britain or France can get something of the effect if he arrives by BEA or Air France and takes the motor launch from the airport across the lagoon, to land by the public gardens at the mouth of the Grand Canal—a striking effect even on the night flight.

I intend that all the principal excursions be done in the morning: museums, churches and galleries are open, and the sunshine helps one to see the pictures. (A lot of the pictures in the churches are dirty and dark: sometimes one can put on a light, and sometimes the sacristan will put on a light, but it is useful to carry a torch.) The best way to do these excursions in the summertime is to start not later than 8 in the morning (earlier if possible); you can then take them at a leisurely pace, have time for sitting down, and for coffee, and still escape the hottest part of the day. If the day is sunny and hot, you can reckon to be on the boat going over to the Lido before noon. I think bathers will want to do the other afternoon excursions on days which are too windy or too cloudy for the Lido, but these excursions are not energetic ones and can be done on the hottest afternoons.

I am indebted to many friends for suggestions and improvements and for acting as guinea-pigs; it is very difficult to tell how a book of this kind is going to work in practice, and I should be grateful to readers for any proposals for improving another edition. I have not quoted from all the works I have consulted: in some cases I have found that a work on Venice does not live up to the writer's more general reputation. My thanks are also due to Mr. Kaffe Fasset who has taken great pains to ensure that his drawings illustrate the text, to Mr. Felix Brenner who was responsible for the physical organisation of the book, and to Miss Juliet Brightmore whose extensive research located the prints and drawings reproduced here. I am particularly indebted to Anna Maria Cicogna for her preface, and for making many suggestions at the proof stage.

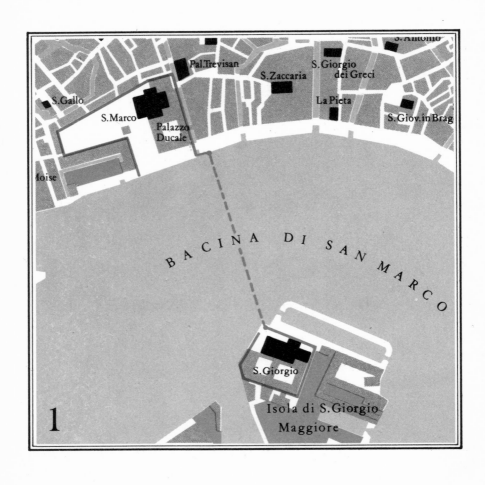

"Streets full of water. Please advise."
Robert Benchley (quoted by Morris).

1

S. Marco – Piazza – Ducal Palace – S. Giorgio

This excursion ends with the island of San Giorgio, which (with luck and an early start) you should reach before lunch. On the island is a group of buildings belonging to the Cini Foundation: they are not generally open to the public, and it is well worth telephoning the secretary of the Foundation for permission to go inside.

Go first, into the Basilica of San Marco, get a ticket for the upper galleries, emerge on the balcony beside the bronze horses, and go to the left-hand corner where a porphyry head sticks up from the balustrade. This is C8 (eighth century) Syrian, believed to represent the Byzantine emperor 'of the broken nose', Justinian II. Just around the corner and on the wall on the left is a Byzantine style madonna probably C13 with votive lamps on either side. This says Hare,

> . . . commemorates the remorse of the Council of Ten for the unjust condemnation of Giovanni Grassi (1611), pardoned ten years after his execution. He swore that the senators who condemned him would all die within the year, and they all obliged him. The lamps were lighted afterwards whenever an execution took place, and the condemned, before mounting the scaffold, turned round to the picture, and repeated the '*Salve Regina*'. The popular tradition of Venice asserts that the two little lamps which constantly burn on this, the south-west side of the church, commemorate the 'Morte Innocente' or *buon anima del fornaretto,* of a baker's boy who (1507) was tried, condemned, and executed for murder— though innocent—because he had picked up the sheath of a dagger with which a murder had been committed in a neighbour- ing calle, and it had been found in his possession.

Lorenzetti says the lamps were left as a thank offering by a sailor saved from a **storm**.

Looking over the edge of the balustrade, you can see the two square pillars of Acre. Believed to be Syrian C5, they are part of the loot brought to Venice from wars in the Near East.

If you look out towards the lagoon and the Island of San Giorgio, with Palladio's church on it, you will see on the left part of the arcaded façade of the Ducal Palace, on the right Sansovino's Library, and, between, the Piazzetta. Just this side of the Ducal Palace is a large gateway—the Porta della Carta, and at the foot of that (on the left) a group of porphyry figures, Egyptian C4, representing the Tetrarchs—the Emperor colleagues of Diocletian. From the ground you can see holes in the helmets where royal crowns were formerly fixed. They are popularly called 'The Moors'.

These notable brothers came from Albania together in a ship laden with great store of riches. After their arrival in Venice which was the place whereunto they were bound, two of them went on shore and left the other two in the ship. They two that were landed entred into a consultation and conspiracy how they might dispatch their other brothers which remained in the ship, to the end they might gaine all the riches to themselues. Whereupon they bought themselues some drugges to that purpose, and determined at a banquet to present the same to their other brothers in a potion or otherwise. Likewise on the other side those two brothers that were left in the shippe whispered secretly amongst themselues how they might make away with their brothers that were landed, that they might get all the wealth to themselues. And thereupon procured means accordingly. At last this was the final issue of those consultations. They that had beene at land presented to their other brothers certaine poysoned drugges at a banquet to the end to kill them, which those brothers did eat and dyed therewith, but not incontinently. For before they ministered a certain poysoned march-pane or some other such thing at the uery same banquet to their brothers that had been at land; both with poysons when they had thoroughly wrought their effects upon both couples, all four dyed shortly after. Whereupon the Signiory of Venice seized upon all their goods as their own, which was the first treasure that euer Venice possessed, and the first occasion of inriching the estate; and in memoriall of that uncharitable and unbrotherly conspiracy, hath erected the pourtraitures of them in porphyrie as I said before in two seuerall couples consulting together.

Coryat.

The two columns at the end of the Piazzetta each carry a statue—one of a lion and one of Saint Theodore.

... S. Theodore (San Todero) martir et cavalier di Dio—standing on a crocodile (by *Pietro Guilombardo* 1329)—the Byzantine saint

18

20

21

who was patron of the Republic before the body of S. Mark was brought from Egypt in 827. Doge Sebastino Ziani (1172–78), having promised any 'onesta grazia' to the man who should safely lift the columns to their places, it was claimed by Nicolo il Barattiere, who demanded that he should be permitted to establish public gambling tables between these pillars. The promise could not be revoked; but to render it of no effect, public executions (previously carried out near San Giovanni in Bragora), were also ordained to be done here so as to make it a place of ill-omen.

Hare.

On the one nearest to the Ducal Palace stands the lion of St. Mark in bronze once *fulgente d'oro* (shining with gold). Originally it was probably a 'chimera' and it has been much discussed, having been considered to be Etruscan by some or Persian of the Sassanid period (IV cent. B.C.) or, according to more recent attributions, a Chinese '*chimera*' the wings having been added to make it a symbol of St. Mark. It was carried off to Paris by the French in 1797 and brought back in 1815 in so bad a state as to require to be partly recast. On the top of the column towards the Library is the marble figure of San Todero (St. Theodore) the Greek saint who was the first patron saint of the Veneto people. The statue is made up of various pieces: the head is of Parian marble, and, according to the most recent studies and comparisons, must be a fine *portrait of Mithridates King of Pontus*; the torso is Roman art of the period of Hadrian with the missing parts added; these latter and the *dragon,* by comparing them with the sculpture on the crowning of St. Mark's show traces of Lombardic art of the first half of the XV cent. The statue actually on the column, on a modern base (dated) is an exact copy of the original which is now kept in the Ducal Palace owing to its very bad state of preservation.

Lorenzetti.

Sansovino, Florentine sculptor and architect, fled the sack of Rome in 1527 and settled in Venice. His grasp of the economics of property development strikes a modern note.

In the year 1529 there were butchers' stalls between the two columns of the Piazza, with a number of small wooden booths, used for the vilest purposes, and a shame as well as deformity to the place, offending the dignity of the Palace and the Piazza, while they could not but disgust all strangers who made their entry into Venice, by the side of San Giorgio.

Sansovino caused these booths and stalls to be removed; he then erected the butchers' shops where they are now, and, adding

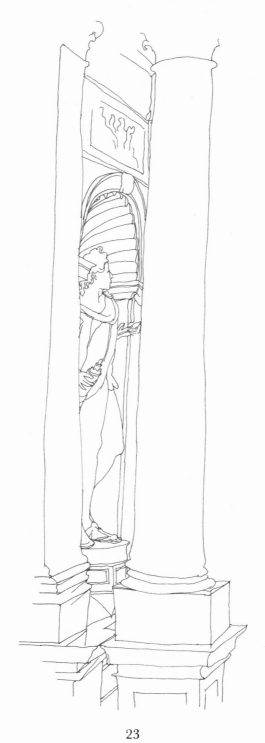

23

to these certain stalls for the dealers in vegetables, he increased the revenues of the Procuranzia by seven hundred ducats yearly, while he beautified the Piazza and the city by the same act. No long time afterwards, he observed that by removing one house in the Merceria (near the clock, and on the way to the Rialto), which paid a rent of twenty-six ducats only, he could open a street into the Spadaria by which the value of the houses and shops all around would be much increased; he took down that house accordingly, thereby adding a hundred and fifty ducats to the income of the Procuranzia. He built the Hostelry of the Pellegrino, moreover, on the same site with another on the Campo Rusulo; and these together brought in four hundred ducats. His buildings in the Pescaria and other part of the city, houses as well as shops, and erected at various times, were also of the utmost utility, and altogether the Procuranzia gained by means of Sansovino, an addition of no less than two thousand ducats per annum, so that they might well hold him in esteem.

Vasari.

Sansovino's old Library (*Libraria Vecchia*) is perhaps one of the most monumental works in Venice. Yet, as Decker puts it,

Venetian buildings retain, above all, anthropomorphous dimensions; they are never monumental in the sense that ancient Roman art, conceived by the Latin spirit, was monumental.

The small building at the foot of the Campanile was also designed by Sansovino. His also are the four bronze statues in the niches, though the terrace and balustrade are a C17 and the bronze gate an C18 addition. All were demolished when the Campanile fell on July 14th, 1902, and reassembled (with new marble facings to the end walls) in 1912 when the Campanile was rebuilt.

In his draperies, his children, and the expression which he gave to his women [Sansovino] never had an equal. The draperies by his hand are, indeed, most delicately beautiful; finely folded, they preserve to perfection the distinction between the nude and draped portions of the form. His children are soft, flexible figures, with none of the muscular development proper only to adults; the little round legs and arms are truly of flesh, and in no wise different to those of Nature herself. The faces of his women are sweet and lovely.

Vasari.

We turn now to the Piazza. Down the left side runs the Old Procuratie (C16) and down the right the New Procuratie (mainly

While staying in Venice in the years 1495-1496 Dürer made a series of studies of Venetians. These two drawings from the Tarocchi series are of an aristocrat with his page, and of the Doge Augustino Barbarigo.

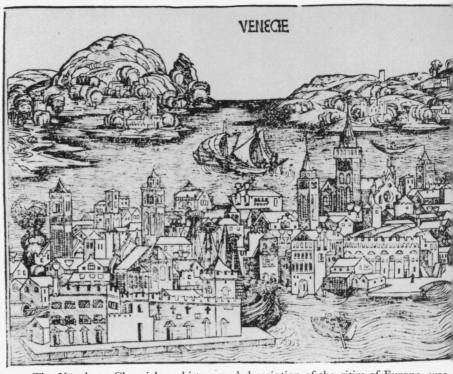

The Nürnberg Chronicle, a history and description of the cities of Europe, was published in Dürer's native town at the very time that he was in Venice.

For two generations the Zucchi family of artists and engravers portrayed the many aspects of Venice. This print was done early in the eighteenth century by Francesco Zucchi (1695-1764) whose son Andrea married the English artist Angelica Kaufman.

Prospetto della Piazza verso il Mare.   F. Zucchi

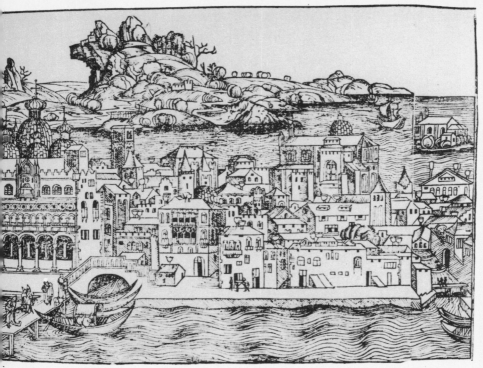

In 1720 Domenico Lovisa published a two-volume collection of engravings by various artists with the title *Gran Teatro delle Più Insigni Prospettive a Venezia* (*Gran Teatro di Venezia*). Fillipo Vasconi (1687-1730) was the editor and a prominent contributor.

Veduta della Piazzetta di S. Marco.

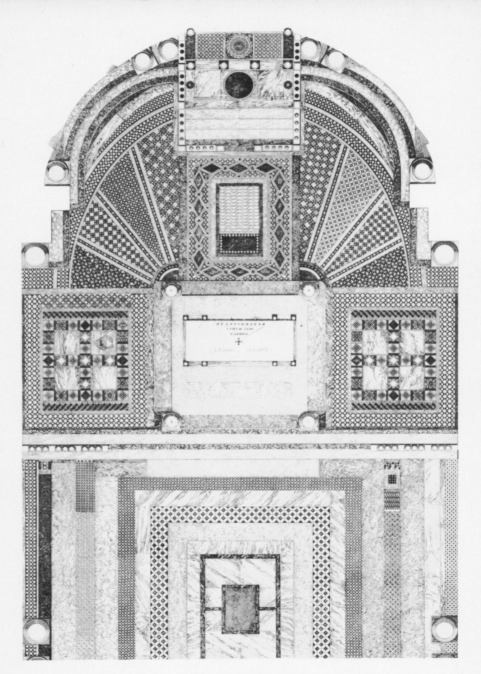

The pavement mosaics around the high altar in San Marco. A detail of an illustration from the book of plates by Giovanni and Luiga Kreutz published in 1843 in a special edition for presentation to the Austrian Emperor Ferdinand on the occasion of his visit.

C17). These were once homes of the Procuratori—important city officers. Between them runs the Ala Napoleonica—a monument of the French occupation. Among the statues on the façade are a number of Roman emperors; the gap in the middle is supposed to have been intended for Napoleon himself. The French continued the looting tradition (as did the Germans in this century) even taking the bronze horses away to Paris. But they were at first greeted as liberators from a useless and effete aristocracy. There is a song still popular in Venice— *la bondina in gondoleta*. (Bands in cafes will play it if asked.) Its heroine is the Countess Querini-Benzoni; a friend of Byron's. When Napoleon was approaching the city, she could be seen (it is said) dancing around a *Tree of Liberty* in front of the Basilica, dressed only in an Athenian tunic.

If you turn back to the Porta della Carta (above the four porphyry Emperors) you will see a marble group representing the Doge Francesco Foscari kneeling before a Venetian lion reading a book. The original was destroyed in the rioting in 1797.

Eighteenth-century Venice was a paradigm of degradation. Her population had declined from 170,000 in her great days to 96,000 in 1797 (though the Venetian Association of Hairdressers still had 852 members). Her trade had vanished, her aristocracy was hopelessly effete, and she depended for her existence upon the tenuous good faith of her neighbours.

No wonder Napoleon swept her aside. The Venetians, temporising and vacillating, offered him no real resistance, and he ended their Republic with a brusque gesture of dismissal: '*Io non voglio più Inquisitori, non voglio più Senato; sarò un Attila per lo stato Veneto*' —'I want no more Inquisitors, no more Senate: I will be an Attila for the Venetian State.' The last of the Doges, limply abdicating, handed his ducal hat to his servant with the febrile comment: 'Take it away, we shan't be needing it again.' (The servant did what he was told, and kept it as a souvenir.) The golden horses of the Basilica, the lion from his pedestal in the Piazetta, many of the treasures of St. Mark's, many of the pictures of the Doges Palace, many precious books and documents—all were taken away to Paris, rather as so many of them had been stolen from Constantinople in the first place. Some diamonds from St. Mark's Treasury were set in Josephine's crown, and a large statue of Napoleon was erected on Sansovino's library building, opposite the Doge's Palace. The last ships of the Venetian Navy were seized to take part in an invasion of Ireland: but when this was cancelled they were sent instead to be sunk by Nelson at Aboukir.

The Great Council itself ended the aristocratic Government of

Venice, by a vote of 512 yeas to 30 nays and 5 blanks, and for the words *'Pax Tibi Marce'*, inscribed on the Venetian lion's open book, there was substituted the slogan 'Rights and Duties of Men and Citizens'. 'At last,' observed a gondolier in a phrase that has become proverbial—'at last he's turned over a new leaf.'

Morris.

The Municipal Band gives concerts in the Piazza in the evening.

I was often suddenly startled towards the end of my meal by the sound of my own overtures; then as I sat at the restaurant window giving myself up to impressions of the music, I did not know which dazzled me most, the incomparable Piazza magnificently illuminated and filled with countless numbers of moving people, or the music that seemed to be borne away in rustling glory to the winds. Only one thing was wanting that might certainly have been expected from an Italian audience: the people were gathered round the band in thousands listening most intently, but no two hands ever forgot themselves so far as to applaud, as the least sign of approbation of Austrian military music would have been looked upon as treason to the Italian Fatherland. All public life in Venice also suffered by this extraordinary rift between the general public and the authorities; this was peculiarly apparent in the relations of the population to the Austrian officers, who floated about publicly in Venice like oil on water. The populace, too, behaved with no less reserve, or one might even say hostility, to the clergy, who were for the most part of Italian origin. I saw a procession of clerics in the vestments passing along the Piazza San Marco accompanied by the people with unconcealed derision.

Wagner.

On the ground, immediately below, stands a stump of a porphyry column, also from a church in the Near East. It was one of two Proclamation Stones—from which the laws of the Republic were proclaimed to the people; the other is in the fruit market by the Rialto Bridge.

In the Piazza itself are, of course,

. . . the pigeons, most celebrated of the Venetian fauna. They are, by tradition, honoured and protected, and to have a roast pigeon lunch you must go down the road to Padua, or better still find yourself a musty trattoria among the Euganean Hills. Some say this is because Dandolo when he stormed Constantinople, sent back the news of the victory by carrier pigeon. Others believe that it arises from an old Palm Sunday custom, when a flock of pigeons was released in the Piazza, those that were caught by the populace being promptly eaten, those that escaped guaranteed permanent immunity—a ceremony that led in the long run, one pigeon

looking very like another, to a safe conduct for them all. Whatever the truth, the pigeons have prospered. They survived some violent epidemics of pigeon-plague, picked up from carrion crows in the Levant, and nowadays never actually die, but merely go out into the lagoon and sink themselves. They are fed twice daily at the public expense, besides being stuffed to excess by indulgent tourists ('those whose ambitions lean in that direction', as Baedeker loftily observes, 'may have themselves photographed covered with the birds').

Morris.

The corn is distributed daily at 9 a.m. and 2 p.m.

We now walk to the opposite end of the exterior gallery, past the bronze horses.

For some decades they were kept at the Arsenal before being put in this place of honour where, about the middle of the XIV century, they were seen and admired by Petrach, who was the first to write in praise of their beauty. They have undergone many restorations in succeeding periods and were traditionally considered to be Greek works of art of the IV–III century B.C. until recently they have been held by Eugenie Strong to be instead Roman works designed to decorate a triumphal arch. The four horses which came from the island of Chios, were sent to Constantinople where they were found by Doge Dandolo on the top of the high Tower of the Hippodrome.

Lorenzetti.

(They) give an intensive animation to the sculptural decoration of St. Mark's. During the centuries when the art of creating equestrian statues was lost, these spirited horses must have been considered as miraculous works.

Decker.

Rising above the *Procuratie Nuove* is the Clock Tower. The clock was made by Paolo and his son Carlo Ronieri of Reggio—as the gilded inscription indicates. The figures on top of the tower strike the hours; during Ascension week other figures emerge from the doors on each side of the Madonna.

On this side of the basilica is the Piazzetta dei Leoncini—the little lions are often ridden by children. Now is a convenient moment to note the whereabouts of:

    (i) Bar Americano—coffee, drinks, cakes, sandwiches cheaper than other cafés hereabouts;

  (ii) Thomas Cook;

 (iii) Venini—some good glassware.

We now return to the interior of the church, at gallery level.

The mosaics are seen at their most brilliant on a bright day with sunlight entering through the west window. It is impossible to study them all: a representative selection may be made as follows:

Early C12: In the cupola nearest the west window—the Cupola of the Pentecost—early C12, Byzantine in style, the Holy Ghost descends to the Apostles.

C12 to C13: Follow the gallery over the right-hand side of the nave: stop at the point where it turns right into the right transept—in front of you (i.e. to the east), on the vault which crosses the transept, mosaics in Ravenna style. Bottom left: Jesus enters Jerusalem.

Early C13: From here you can see some of the figures of the central cupola (The Ascension dome): this is a Venetian version of Byzantine mannerist style remarkable, as Demus says, for its 'agitated movements, swirling draperies with plastic islands surrounded by flowing folds, distorted faces and dynamic compositions'. On your way to this spot you passed the *Prayer in the Garden* on your right. It is the lower scene on the wall of the right aisle. Here the Byzantine background has begun to make way for landscape.

Late C13: Turn now into the right transept. On the wall on the right (i.e. the west wall) the lower scene tells the legend of the *Finding of the Body of St. Mark*.

> In this is represented with ingenious art, the interior of the Basilica, where the episodes here described took place. The tradition relates how in 1063, when the building of the new temple was begun, the body of the Evangelist was, during the building, jealously hidden; afterwards the traces were lost and every search having proved fruitless, special fasts and services were held. In the scene at the left: (a) *The Doge, the Signoria, the Clergy and the People take part in the services celebrated in St. Mark's for help to find the body of the Evangelist*. After this, by a wonderful miracle, St. Mark revealed the place where his body had been deposited and from the pilaster beside the present Altar of the Sacrament an arm appeared destroying part of the marble facing which hid it. Indeed in the mosaic to the right, (b) *The Bishop, the Doge, the Procuratori and the People* are present in surprise at the miracle. This happened, according to the pious tradition, on the 25th June 1094.
>
> *Lorenzetti.*

If you turn round and look over the balustrading down into the church you will be facing the Altar of the Sacrament. On the left of this altar is the pillar in question: a panel and a lamp mark the spot.

One other area (mid C13) merits special mention: it is the arch immediately to the east of the Pentecost Cupola. *Jesus descending into Limbo*—the upper scene—can be seen from this side: it is worth going round to the other side to view the *Crucifixion*. The great period of mosaic appears to have ended with the C13; you will notice many examples of later periods—by which time the art of mosaic had become largely an exercise in ingenuity.

The galleries themselves were designed, according to the Eastern custom, to accommodate the women during the ceremonies. The galleries on either side of the nave have parapets made up of carved and pierced panels C6–C11. The endless variety of columns and capitals can also be seen from here.

We can now go down to see the lower floor of the cathedral. We may start by looking first at the exterior.

The base of the central standard is a convenient resting place. On it is a small profile of a C16 Doge, in the shape of a medallion. The central arch of the basilica displays a miniature history of the development of Romanesque sculpture: the inmost arch is early C13, the middle later, and the outer arch early C14.

> Now the first broad characteristic of the building, and the root of nearly every other important peculiarity in it, is its confessed *incrustation*. It is the purest example in Italy of the great school of architecture in which the ruling principle is the incrustation of brick with more precious materials, and it is necessary, before we proceed to criticise any one of its arrangements, that the reader should carefully consider the principles which are likely to have influenced, or might legitimately influence, the architects of such a school, as distinguished from those whose designs are to be executed in massive materials. This incrusted school appears insincere at first to a Northern builder, because, accustomed to build with solid blocks of freestone, he is in the habit of supposing the external superficies of a piece of masonry to be some criterion of its thickness. But, as soon as he gets acquainted with the incrusted style, he will find that the Southern builders had no intention to deceive him. He will see that every slab of facial marble is fastened to the next by a confessed *rivet,* and that the joints of the armour are so visibly and openly accommodated to the contours of the substance within that he has no more right to complain of treachery than a savage would have, who, for the first time in his life seeing a man in armour, had supposed him to be made of solid steel. Acquaint him with the customs of chivalry, and with the uses of the coat of mail, and he ceases to accuse of dishonesty either the panoply or the knight.
>
> *Ruskin.*

Venice took her role as heir to a part of the Roman Empire very seriously. And this accounts for the method of decorating the exterior of San Marco—and much else besides—in Veneto-Byzantine architecture. Many of the elements in the decorative scheme are Byzantine—notably the use of sculpture as surface ornament and not, as was normal elsewhere in Europe, to express the structure. But no parallel to the abundance of columns and marble cladding is to be found on any other Byzantine building of this period. Archaeologists have discovered behind these decorations the mid-twelfth-century brick façade which, somewhat surprisingly, was decorated not with round headed but with pointed arches and arcading. Thus, when the rest of Europe was developing the Gothic style, Venice was turning back to the ancient world for inspiration. Apparently this lavish use of marble was a conscious attempt to revive the splendours of ancient Rome—though the architect looked back no further than to the Early Christian period. It was, however, by such a return to a form of classicism—also reflected in domestic architecture where the two-story portico became popular—that Venice triumphantly proclaimed her succession to the Roman Empire, if no more than a 'quarter and half a quarter' of it.

On the main façade the carvings are arranged in a clear iconographic programme to stress the church's function as a national shrine. The basic construction is that of a vast triumphal arch with five openings. In the spandrels between the arches there are six relief carvings. That on the far left represents Hercules carrying the Erymanthean boar, a Roman work of the third century, that on the far right is a Venetian imitation of it carved one thousand years later. Hercules was supposed to have been the original tribal hero of the Veneti from whom the Venetians claimed descent, he had an allegorical role as the Saviour conquering evil, he was also recognised as the type of hero protector. The next two reliefs, reading inwards—Venetian carvings after Byzantine prototypes—represent the Virgin and the Archangel of the Annunciation both of whom were regarded as protectors of the ruler of the state. The two central reliefs represent Saints who were warriors and thus the protectors of warriors, St. Demetrius and St. George—the first a late twelfth-century Byzantine carving and the second a Venetian imitation of it. . . .

Honour.

It is worth looking closely at the arch at the extreme left of the façade (the **Porta di San Alipio**). The mosaic, C13, shows the church as it was then, and the body of St. Mark being carried into it. Needing a relic and a patron saint of more consequence than the Greek San Todero, the Venetians stole the body from Alexandria in 829. The other

mosaics were later replaced, but most of them can be seen in Bellini's
Procession in the Accademia (p. 99). The reliefs of figures and vines
on the outer arch are early C13. Below are five pierced screens of
Byzantine window form. The lintel appears to be C5 or C6.

The reliefs which decorate the lintel as a revetment consisting
of eleven pieces do not, at present, make good sense iconographically speaking: the original ensemble must have been
larger, the present one being only the remnant assembled above
one door, of a programme that was made to fit two or three doors;
but the left corner piece of the revetment is still 'in situ', and,
what is more important, it furnishes conclusive evidence that it
was expressly made for its actual position: the framing pillar on the
left-hand side of the relief is inclined towards the right, in order to
fit the slant of the adjoining architrave. As this architrave is a part
of the façade incrustation which can be dated between ca. 1230
and ca. 1260, the lintel reliefs must have been made at the same
time.

However, the reliefs of the Porta di St. Alipio are datable not
only on technical grounds; they show the imprint of the thirteenth
century also in their iconography and in their style. The 'her-
aldic' composition of the miracle of Cana, with two servants
pouring water symmetrically on either side of Christ, the shape of
the Child's cradle in the Annunciation to the shepherds, the
implements carried by the two deacons at either end, their
costumes, with the cross-decorated stole (orarium) hanging down
over their left shoulders, the numerous misunderstandings in the
arrangement of the draperies and the character of the ornamental
details are all proof that the reliefs are not genuine early Christian
works but more or less clever thirteenth century imitations of
models which may have been ivories or wood carvings of the late
fifth or the sixth century.
Demus.

We can enter by the central arch. On the floor—marble mosaics
C11–C12 and a red lozenge of stone, traditionally the spot where
Barbarossa submitted to Pope Alexander III in 1177. On the ceiling,
fine C13 mosaics: the last cupola on the right is the earliest and best
preserved. The series begins in the dome on the extreme right with the
Creation of the World.

It has been known since the eighties of the last century, when
J. J. Tikkanen published his discovery, that the Old Testament
mosaics of the Narthex or Atrium of San Marco in Venice are, at
least in their greater part, more or less faithful copies of an illuminated manuscript of the type of the Cotton Genesis in the British
Museum. It would, of course, be wrong to expect from the
Venetian mosaicists of the thirteenth century slavish reproductions

The interior court of the Ducal Palace in 1741 by Michele Marieschi (1710-1743). The Doge Alvise Mocenigo IV receiving the foreign ambassadors in the Sala Collegio, 1763. An engraving by Giovanni Batista Brustoloni from a drawing by Canaletto.

Everyday market-place scenes which persisted for centuries and have only recently died out. These, drawn and engraved by Gaetano Zompini (1702-1778) in 1750, are the Punch and Judy show, the fortune teller, the rat-catcher and the seller of theatrical-box keys.

of their more than 700 year old models; Tikkanen has shown that they retained a certain independence in the selection of the scenes to be included in their programme and that they altered the prototypes as regards position and spacing of figures, coloring, and movement, even going so far as to break up some of the old compositions and making up new ones from their component parts. Forlati's soundings make it likely that the preparatory brush drawings (sinopie) were closer to the model than the finished mosaics. But even so, the mosaics are close enough to dispel any doubt that the Venetian mosaicists of the thirteenth century had both the intention and the ability to bring about in their work a close approximation to early sixth century iconography and style.

All this goes to show that there was a strong archaizing current in Venetian art, manifesting itself in the collecting and exhibiting of early spoils, in the copying and imitating of early Christian works of painting and sculpture; a current that must have been strong enough to result in the unparalleled ability of Venetian masters to speak fluently, as it were, a foreign language of style and meaning. Now, what can have been the driving forces behind this movement which goes far beyond the usual trends of archaism in medieval art? The answer lies in the very special situation of Venice, both geographically and historically. Venice had, to begin with, no hinterland, at least in the earlier stages of its civic development. No deeply ingrained tendencies were present which might have prevented the Venetian artists from giving themselves over to the imitation of foreign and antiquated forms. But Venice lacked more than a hinterland: it lacked a past. It had appeared comparatively late in the history of the Mediterranean world. Being without a past was, however, in the Middle Ages very much like being a man without his shadow—like Chamisso's Peter Schlemihl. To cure this defect, the statesmen of the Middle Ages developed a remedy—the same that is being used even today by states and individuals: if one had no past, one could always fake one. In a way, this was easier than it is now. The forgers of the Middle Ages were not hampered as we are, by existing records, proofs, and counterproofs. They could fake freely and to measure.

This is what the Venetians did, at least from the eleventh century onwards, when the need arose to bolster up their slowly developed independence, especially in ecclesiastic matters. An intricate web of forgeries was fabricated (and borrowed) by which Grado, the Metropolitan See of the National Church of Venice, was made to appear as the legitimate successor of Aquileia which, in its turn, traced its origin, by forged documents and legends, back to St. Hermagoras and through him, to the Holy Mark himself. The church of the Evangelist, the very center of Venetian political and religious life, could not be antedated: the date of the transfer of the Patron Saint's relics from Alexandria to Venice in 828–829 and of the subsequent erection of his first church in Rialto was too well established; but the church could be given an aura of venerability by making it a 'simile' of the old and venerable Church of the Holy Apostles in Constantinople where, as in San Marco itself, the 'pignora imperii' were kept. Venice resurrected with this also a time-hallowed Italian tradition that can be followed back to St. Ambrose's foundation of Apostles' churches from Milan to Rouen, Aquileia, and Fondi.

The building of the first San Marco, from 830 onwards, after the pattern of the Holy Apostles was, as far as we know, the earliest instance of conscious archaism in Venice. The second building, at the end of the eleventh century, improved on its predecessor which had, in all probability, wooden cupolas. Now, from 1063 onwards, the church was vaulted and built in brick as one of the most successful imitations of a famous model that the history of architecture knows. But, even so, it was not perfect: it lacked a decoration to vie with the mosaics of the Constantinople church. The early thirteenth century remedied this.

Demus.

Right at the opposite end of the atrium (past the postcard stall and round the corner to the right) is the *Moses* cupola. The ten scenes depict incidents from the life of Moses in a manner quite remote from the pseudo-archaic *Genesis* cupola.

Just before you enter the church there is a stall selling tickets for the *Pala d'Oro*. This is the moment to buy one.

Let us enter the church. It is lost in still deeper twilight, to which the eye must be accustomed for some moments before the form of the building can be traced; and then there opens before us a vast cave, hewn out into the form of a Cross, and divided into shadowy aisles by many pillars. Round the domes of its roof the light enters only through narrow apertures like large stars; and here and there a ray or two from some far-away casement wanders into the darkness, and casts a narrow phosphoric stream upon the waves of marble that heave and fall in a thousand colours along the floor. What else there is of light is from torches, or silver lamps, burning ceaselessly in the recesses of the chapels; the roof sheeted with gold, and the polished walls covered with alabaster, give back at every curve and angle some feeble gleaming to the flames; and the glories round the heads of the sculptured saints flash out upon us as we pass them and sink again into the gloom. Under foot and over head, a continual succession of crowded imagery, one picture passing into another, as in a dream; forms beautiful and terrible mixed together—dragons and serpents, and ravening beasts of prey, and graceful birds that in the midst of them drink from running fountains and feed from bases of crystal; the passions and the pleasures of human life symbolised together, and the mystery of its redemption; for the mazes of interwoven lines and changeful pictures lead always at last to the Cross, lifted and carved in every place and upon every stone; sometimes with the serpent of eternity wrapt round it, sometimes with doves beneath its arms, and sweet herbage growing forth from its feet; but conspicuous most of all on the great rood that crosses the church before the altar, raised in bright blazonry against the shadow of the apse.

Ruskin.

In the use of significant geometrical figures—the square, the circle and the cross—and the mystic relationship between the proportions, it answers the Byzantine passion for symbolism and the Byzantine belief in the laws of harmony and sanctity of mathematics, 'the highest of the sciences'. Nevertheless, it is essentially a Byzantine church with Italian decorations and nothing like it was ever built in the eastern Empire. The original effect was quite different and much more outspokenly Byzantine. There were many more windows and there were galleries above the aisles so that light flooded into the whole central area making a much stronger contrast with the surrounding shade. With their passion for surface decoration, the Venetians walled up many windows to make room for additional mosaics. This made the area under the galleries so dangerously dark that their floors had to be removed, leaving only the strange cat-walks you see today.

Honour.

It is all so quiet and sad and faded and yet all so brilliant and living. The strange figures in the mosaic pictures, bending with the curve of niche and vault, stare down through the glowing dimness; the burnished gold that stands behind them catches the light on its little uneven cubes. St. Mark's owes nothing of its character to the beauty of proportion or perspective; there is nothing grandly balanced or far-arching; there are no long lines nor triumphs of the perpendicular. The church arches indeed, but arches like a dusky cavern. Beauty of surface, of tone, of detail, of things near enough to touch and kneel upon and lean against—it is from this the effect proceeds. In this sort of beauty the place is incredibly rich, and you may go there every day and find afresh some lurking pictorial nook. You grow fond even of the old benches of red marble, partly worn away by the breeches of many generations and attached to

41

the base of those wide pilasters of which the precious plating, delightful in its faded brownness, with a faint grey bloom upon it, bulges and yawns a little with honourable age.

Henry James.

Beside the first column on the right there is a porphyry stoup supported on Roman fragment C2. Through the door behind is the Baptistry, and opposite the entrance the Funeral Monument of Doge Andrea Dandolo mid C14—see the reliefs on the front of the sarcophogi (the dove especially). Turning right we reach the *Cappella Zen*, remodelled C16. The mannerist figures on and around the tomb are of representative interest.

Up in the central cupola the nude angels and larger figures indicate the Byzantine debt to Hellenistic models. The later mosaic of Salome (on the left of the lunette over the entrance door) owes more to the Gothic; she is pictured as a fashionably dressed woman of the mid C14.

Back in the main body of the church, we move up the right aisle. The floor mosaics deserve attention. In front of the rood screen look at the little arches and pilasters (C11) which decorate the base of the chancel. Admission to the Pala d'Oro is at the right of the high altar. The C10–C12 enamels were taken from Byzantium. They are set in a screen which reached its present form in C14. (Restored mid C19.) If you stand in front of the high altar and facing it, you will see on the vault over the gallery on the right a series of mosaics illustrating episodes from the life of St. Mark. Demus takes the last—the body of the saint welcomed by the Doge, clergy and people—as an example of the archaising trends and tendencies of the mid C13 in Venice: it is an adapted copy of a C6 mosaic, the dedicatory panel of Justinian, in San Vitale, Ravenna. On either side of the chancel (behind you at this point) are two little galleries decorated with high renaissance reliefs by Sansovino—only really visible if the day is bright.

Over the high altar is the richly decorated ciborium supported on four columns: these are better known examples of the same tendency. They appear to be works of early Christian character both as regards style and iconography, but certainly the front pair and probably also the back pair are now believed to be works of the C13.

Left transept, east side, the altar of the Virgin (C17) contains an image of the Virgin called La Nicopeia also taken by the Venetians from Byzantium at the time of the fourth crusade.

Returning from the Pala d'Oro, we are back in the right transept: the same ticket gains admission to the Treasury. Turning to the right inside the door we come upon a number of precious objects, of which the Byzantine are the most interesting.

. . . it is important to remember that in Byzantium, as in China, there was no dividing line between the major and minor arts. It would not be going too far to say that all Byzantine arts, including architecture, aspired to the jewel-like delicacy and richness of an enamelled reliquary. In the Treasury there is a twelfth-century reliquary of gold and silver in the form of a church*—it should be regarded as an ideal of what a church should look like rather than the model of a building. Had Byzantine architects been able to build with gold and silver and precious stones they would undoubtedly have done so.

Honour.

At the extreme end of the left transept in the Chapel of the Madonna of the Males (Mascoli). The relief on the altar front—two angels bearing censers—shows Tuscan influence. The mosaics (C15) are late but fine.

On the way out we walk over some fine mosaics of birds in the left aisle, and pass the lower pulpit (late C13) on which is superimposed a pulpit of later date owing much to South Italian and Islamic styles.

We now come back into the Piazza. This is a good moment for a rest —perhaps some coffee—and some more general observations.

The palaces of Venice, when they need support, are strengthened by the injection of concrete into their foundations, as a dentist squeezes a filling into a rotting but still useful tooth: this entails the building of a water-tight caisson around the house, and the Municipality contributes half the cost. About thirty of the Grand Canal palaces have been treated. The Basilica is constantly attended by its own private consultant, the resident engineer, successor to a long line of Architects to St. Mark's. This learned and devoted man knows every inch of his church, and spends his life devising ways of strengthening it without spoiling its antique irregularities. He has a staff of nearly forty men working all the year round, and a mosaic workshop manned by twelve skilled craftsmen. He is always experimenting and has in particular perfected a means of replacing broken chips of mosaic in the ceiling by cutting through the masonry above and inserting the precious fragments from behind.

Morris.

Few of the sightseers who flock to Venice every year from all over the world get to see and understand the real plight of the city. In 15 years—from 1951 to 1966—over 50,000 of its residents fled

* This is to be found in a free-standing show-case on the right, bottom shelf.

from decaying, unhealthy and water-logged buildings to the mainland. The population dropped from 176,000 to 121,000, while that of the mainland areas of Porto Marghera and Mestre increased from 96,000 to 193,000. Rather than live in Venice, several thousand Venetians prefer to commute every day between their homes on the mainland and their jobs in the city. Life in the poorer parts of the Lagoon city has become one long struggle against dampness, crumbling buildings, stench, and rats.

The discovery of America, which switched the focus of European interest from the Mediterranean to the Atlantic, started the decline of Venice. The Venetian Republic was conquered and given to Austria by Napoleon in 1797, and was annexed to the new kingdom of Italy in 1866. The neglect of the great sea walls on the seaward side of the outer islands enclosing the Lagoon dates back to 1866. At the same time, the Magistero Delle Acque, the all-powerful official body which was responsible for the upkeep of the sea walls and of the Lagoon in general, was deprived of most of its powers and tasks which were then spread out among various national Ministries.

For still-unexplained geological reasons, the whole of the Po Valley (Venice is sited at its tip) is subsiding. It is difficult to find a church tower anywhere in the valley which has not become a leaning one to some degree. The subsidence of the Lagoon bed enables sea water to rush into the Lagoon with the high tides. The 'acqua alta' (high water) days, particularly in autumn, used to be an exceptional event. However, they have now become frequent, with water not only flooding St. Mark's Square, but lapping the goods displayed in shop windows. A special siren alarm service has been set up to give warning when a high incoming tide is reported.

The idea of endowing Venice with an industrial area got under way some 50 years ago. Porto Marghera was built on the mainland shore of the Lagoon, and was followed by another. Now, a third one of about 8,000 acres is planned. It will be brought about by filling-in the marsh islets known locally as 'barene'. Ships going to Porto Marghera cross the Lagoon in a deep-water channel which passes in front of St. Mark's Square. A new deep-water channel from the Malamocco-Lido sea outlet of the Lagoon directly to Porto Marghera is being dredged and is nearly complete. There are fears that this channel will hasten the inrush into the Lagoon of the high tides, just as it is feared that the filling-in of the 'barene' will deprive the Lagoon of a sort of buffer against high tides which used to exhaust themselves harmlessly flooding the marsh islets. Reservations are also held that a third industrial area, entailing the pumping of more fresh water from wells, will hasten the subsidence of the Lagoon bed.   *Tumiati.*

Venice rose and lives on the water: for this reason its water-ways are as important in its life as the network of its streets. The internal Rii (canals), filled with shallow water about two metres deep and not very wide (from 4 to 5 metres), used by gondolas, launches, and shallow draft boats, are spanned by *Bridges* that connect both banks, often flanked by long narrow streets—the fondamenta that run close to the foundations of the houses. The bridges, originally flat with planks, suitable for horse traffic, a means of transport still used by Venetians up to the fifteenth century, then later built of stone and brick, arched and with balustrades. The two largest tracts of water are, however, called Canals: the *Giudecca Canal* which is very large and the *Grand Canal* which, with a double curve divides the city into two parts anciently called: *de citra e de ultra,* that is on this and that side of the Canal in respect to the Piazza San Marco; besides being used by craft of every kind and shape, it is spanned by three large bridges: the *Rialto Bridge,* the oldest (XVI cent.) almost half-way down it, made of stone, the Academy Bridge in wood, and the Railway Bridge in stone (Eugenio Miozzi 1932). The two shores are, besides, connected by numerous ferries, mooring places for gondolas and for the carrying of people from one side of the canal to the other.

Although the water-ways have, of necessity, been developed, it must not be thought, as is erroneously done by non-Venetians, that to go round Venice one has absolutely to use boats. On the contrary many picturesque and characteristic corners hidden in the interior of the city can only be reached by penetrating the intricate maze of its alleyways: those are the *calli,* some of which are so narrow as to allow one person to pass with difficulty, and made still more dark by buildings jutting out (to gain space), sustained by wooden joists, the *barbacani,* which almost form a covering to them. Quite often, however, the maze of alleys is interrupted by spacious areas of open ground, the *campi,* so called because they were once grassy; these generally stretch out before a church and one or more *vere da pozzo* (well-heads) are almost never lacking. The one of San Marco was called a *piazza* because it is more beautiful and spacious, and the two smaller ones adjoining it *piazzette,* just as only the embankment that runs along beside the Pool of San Marco was given the name *Riva degli Schiavoni. Corti* and *campielli* are smaller open spaces, less than the *campi.* The medium width streets, flanked with houses and shops are called *ruga* or *rughetta.* A *rio terrà* is, instead, a *rio interrato* (filled-in canal) and turned into a street. The first streets to be paved are called *salizzade. Ramo* is a small trace of a street connecting two bigger streets. Little sorts of ponds where the rain-water stagnated, later filled in, were called by the very old name of *piscine.* Last of all the *sottoportici* are the covered passageways

45

or more or less narrow passages, opened for the convenience of the public, beneath private homes.

Apart from a few exceptions the old nomenclature of the streets has been maintained more or less unaltered. The characteristic denominations in Venetian dialect have been preserved, written in big black letters on a plaster background. They are names derived from the neighbourhoods, very often of the Patron Saint of the parish, so that we might say that by wandering round Venice we can learn and repeat most of the religious calendar. Sometimes these names recall the aristocratic family that lived nearby or some characteristic oddity of the spot. At times, however, the names have suffered strange incomprehensible transformations such as: *San Trovaso*, a combination of two names of Gervasio and Protasio; *San Stae*, a transformation of Sant' Eustachio; *San Marcuola*, the fusion of the two names Sant Ermagora and Fortunato; *San Lio*, an abbreviation of San Leone; *Sant' Aponal*, from Sant Apollinare, etc.

Lorenzetti.

We now walk towards the Lagoon, into the Piazetta. The C16 building on the right is Sansovino's Library. It reminds us that the Venetians were not intellectuals: Venice was famous for its printers, not writers. The last thing suggested by this splendid and showy civic monument is anything which could be described as 'bookish'.

Sansovino had completely adapted his style and manner to the genius of the place, the brilliant light of Venice, which is reflected by the lagoons, and dazzles the eyes by its splendour. It may seem a little pedantic to anatomize such a festive and simple building, but to look at it carefully may help us to see how skilled these masters were in weaving a few simple elements into ever-new patterns. The lower storey, then, with its vigorous Doric order of columns, is in the most orthodox classical manner. Sansovino had closely followed the rules of building which the Colosseum exemplified. He adhered to the same tradition when he arranged the upper storey in the Ionic order, carrying a so-called 'attic' crowned with a balustrade and topped by a row of statues. But instead of letting the arched openings between the orders rest on pillars, as had been the case on the Colosseum, Sansovino supported them by another set of small Ionic columns, and thus achieved a rich effect of interlocked orders. With his balustrade, garlands and sculptures he gave the building something of the appearance of tracery such as had been used on the Gothic façades of Venice.

Gombrich.

46

47

The Library contains book bindings, illuminated codexes, and early printed books. In the vestibule, Titian's *Wisdom*.

> In painting . . . a greater effect of reality is chiefly a matter of light and shadow, to be obtained only by considering the canvas as an enclosed space, filled with light and air, through which the objects are seen. There is more than one way of getting this effect, but Titian attains it by the almost total suppression of outlines, by the harmonizing of his colours, and by the largeness and vigour of his brushwork. In fact, the old Titian was, in his way of painting, remarkably like the best French masters at the end of the nineteenth century. This makes him only the more attractive, particularly when with handling of this kind he combined the power of creating forms of beauty such as he has given us in '*Wisdom*'.
>
> *Berenson.*

The Hall is remarkable for its ceiling of real gold. Pictures on each side of the door: Veronese, *Two Philosophers*.

If you look at the Library from the waterfront you will see the façade of the former Mint (*Zecca*). The word 'sequin' appears to be derived from the *Zecchini*—gold ducats—minted in Venice. A collection of Venetian coins is housed in the Correr museum; the Zecca contains ancient books and manuscripts.

We now turn to the façade of the Ducal Palace.

> The outer walls rest upon the sturdy pillars of open colonnades, which have a more stumpy appearance than was intended, owing to the raising of the pavement in the piazza.
>
> *Hare.*

Pass in front of the Ducal Palace, to the bridge. Byron's line beginning the fourth canto of *Childe Harold*,

I stood in Venice, on the Bridge of Sighs

presumably means that he stood in Venice on this bridge—the Bridge of Straw (Ponte di Paglia)—and contemplated the Bridge of Sighs. The view is deservedly famous. The bridge is grimly elegant: it contains dark passages, lit by gratings, connecting the palace with the prison. It is worth going over the Straw Bridge, turning immediately left and looking through the arcades of the Palazzo. From here you can also see the relief of the *Drunkenness of Noah* on the corner of the Palazzo; two sons cover his nakedness, the other son is represented on the other side of the arch.

. . . in several cases, the sculptor has shown the under sides of the leaves turned boldly to the light, and has literally carved every rib and vein upon them in relief; not merely the main ribs which sustain the lobes of the leaf, and actually project in nature, but the irregular and sinuous veins which chequer the membranous tissues between them, and which the sculptor has represented conventionally as relieved like the others, in order to give the vine-leaf its peculiar tessellated effect upon the eye. . . .   *Ruskin.*

Now come back in front of the Palazzo and return to the Piazzetta: the gothic reliefs on the capitals merit, as Ruskin advised, careful examination (though a number of them have been replaced by late C19 facsimiles).

Under the arcading on the Piazzetta side is an illuminating tablet. The first duty of the Venetian nobleman was to the state: if he failed in his duty he was punished. In no other country in the world, as Hare remarks, does one see tablets set up in the walls of public edifices, with inscriptions which do not praise but condemn. Here we read that Girolamo Loredan and Giovanni Contarini were banished for having ceded the fortress of Tenedo to the Turks, with its arms and munitions, causing grave injury to Christianity, and to their country.

At the end of the arcade we come once again to the Porta della Carta: on the right, the *Judgment of Solomon*; on the pillar, the astrological references on the capital; in front, the C15 *Giants' Stairs*—a magnificent gesture in incrusted marble, now topped by Sansovino's guardian figures of the 'giants' Mars and Neptune, monumental in size, but in relaxed mannerist attitudes. We enter the courtyard through the Foscari Porch (*Arco Foscari*): the charming Adam and Eve figures are by Antonio Rizzo, the architect of the Giants' Stairs. It is only fair to say at this stage that the inside of the Palazzo is a bit of an ordeal; there are however some fine things, and by being extremely selective, I think it is possible to enjoy them—though other authors are less encouraging: one American attributes the 'verveless' pictures to the 'gangs of restorers' from the C18 onwards, which other collections escaped.

At the time of writing, the route through the Palazzo is as follows:

First Floor Gallery
Hall of the Inferior Chancery
Room of the Provveditori della Milizia da Mar
First Hall of the Avogaria

After the division arch, on the wall of the arch, up on the left: Bombelli: *Portraits of Three Avogadori.*

50

These full-lengths, which were to become so frequent and popular in 18th Century Venice, derive in the first place from the big votive paintings of the Renaissance, in which senators and doges solemnly kneel before an altar or a divine personage and in which they personify Venice. Everything in those pictures emphasized the hieratic; the grave profile and dignified gesture, the rich official clothes, all subduing the personality so that each man becomes only a symbol of the Republic itself.

But in the later work, the divine element has disappeared.

By the time of Bombelli's double portrait of the *Avogadori Pietro Garzoni and Francesco Benzon,* painted about 1683–84, we have only the undramatic Dove in the sky above the two men, one of whom rather shyly indicates its presence. The picture is frankly a double portrait, a vividly human one in which the celestial appurtenance is barely a distraction; and in other portraits of similar personages by Bombelli even this last faint intrusion is replaced by a plain setting about the figures.

Levey.

Golden Staircase
Doges' Apartments
Hall of the Scarlatti
Hall of the Escutcheons
Hall of the Philosophers

Over last but one door on left: Titian fresco of *Saint Christopher.*

Erizzo Room
Grimani Hall

On wall facing windows: Carpaccio: *Winged Lion* Passant. On its right, C15 bust of Doge Francesco Foscari, remnant of the group over the Porta della Carta.

Square Saloon
Hall of the Four Doors

Over the window on the canal: G. B. Tiepolo: *Neptune Bearing Treasures to Venice.* Next but one on the right: Titian: *Doge Grimani Kneeling before Faith.*

Hall of the Ante-College

On wall facing windows: Vernonese: *Rape of Europa.*
On wall beside window: Tintoretto: *Bacchus and Ariadne.*

College Hall

The roof is entirely by Paul Veronese, and the traveller who really loves painting ought to get leave to come to this room whenever he chooses, and should pass the sunny summer mornings there again and again . . . He will not otherwise enter so deeply into the heart of Venice.

Ruskin.

Over the exit door: Tintoretto: *Marriage of Saint Catherine.*

> Senate Hall
> Ante-Chapel
> Chapel
> Hall of the Council of Ten
> Room of the Bussola
> Hall of the Three Chiefs

Ceiling: left rectangle on window side: Veronese: *Punished Forger.*

> Hall of the Inquisitors of State
> Room of the Arms
> Hall of Gattamelata
> Morosini Hall
> Bragadin Hall
> Lobby of Small Staircase
> Ante-chamber of 'Great Council'
> Hall of Old Civil Quarantiae
> Guariento's Room
> The 'Great Council' Hall

Wall over throne: Tintoretto: *Paradiso.*

I believe this is, on the whole, Tintoret's 'chef-d'oeuvre'; though it is so vast that no one takes the trouble to read it, and therefore less wonderful pictures are preferred to it. . . . In the Paradise of Tintoret, the angel is seen in the distance driving Adam and Eve out of the garden. Not, for Tintoret, the leading to the gate with consolation and counsel. His strange ardour of conception is seen here as everywhere. Full speed they fly, the angel and the human creatures; the angel, wrapt in an orb of light, floats on, stooped forward in his fierce flight, and does not touch the ground; the chastised creatures rush before him in abandoned terror. All this might have been invented by another, though in other hands it would assuredly have been offensive; but one circumstance which completes the story, could have been thought of by none but Tintoret. The angel casts a shadow before him towards Adam and Eve.

Ruskin.

In the oval on the ceiling above the *Paradiso,* Veronese: *Apotheosis of Venice.*

The matronly personification of Venice is shown enthroned in clouds (in which the supporting goddesses recline) in front of a vast arcade. On the balcony below, a group of ladies and gentlemen together with their children and pets, show a mild and aristocratic interest, and lower still two soldiers on charging stallions attempt to control the crowd. . . . The general effect of Veronese's painting is decidedly Baroque. Incompletely so, perhaps, for only in the lowest zone is there any real movement, while the whole lacks that display of emotion which was to be such an important element in infusing unity into the great decorative schemes of the succeeding century. Nevertheless, the elaborate illusionism of the architecture and the tremendous confidence and swagger of the conception produces an effect of momentarily stunning the senses which is altogether Baroque. And yet when we recover from the shock and bring ourselves to examine the work in detail, the ingredients are very much the same as in the classical Renaissance-like composition of the Feast* . . . The figures have the same nobility and the same air of detachment. In principle, the *Triumph* is simply the *Feast* seen not at eye-level but from a great distance below.

If the seeming-Renaissance can be transformed so easily into the seeming-Baroque it is clear that the barriers between the two are less final than is usually supposed. . . . There was at this time no fundamental antagonism between the classical design of the Renaissance and the Baroque system . . . the former was the perfect vehicle of expression for placid subjects and the latter for animated ones.

Gould.

Second Hall of the Avogaria.

On the entrance wall: Giovanni Bellini: *Jesus Supported by Virgin and Saints.*

The Church from the first took account of the influence of colour as well as of music upon the emotions. From the earliest times it employed mosaic and painting to enforce its dogmas and relate its legends, not merely because this was the only means of reaching people who could neither read nor write but also because it instructed them in a way which, far from leading to critical

*In the Accademia, p.93

In 1630 the Senate voted funds for the building of Santa Maria della Salute.
Longhena's design was accepted a year later and Marco Boschini made this
engraving from Longhena's model (reproduced in 1720 in the *Gran Teatro di
Venezia*) to show how the opening ceremony might look. The building was in fact
completed in 1681 and consecrated in 1687.

From 1741 until about 1744 Canaletto drew and etched a number of Venetian scenes. These views have a vitality and freshness not found in engravings done from his work by other printers. Above, the bird-market scene on the Mole between the two columns shows, in the background, the striped-awning covered barge where convicted prisoners were kept until deportation. The lower view of the Prison looks down the Riva degli Schiavoni.

The crenallated buildings which housed both the department of health and the public granary, in this plate from the *Gran Teatro di Venezia*, was pulled down during the Napoleonic occupation. The site is now a public garden, with trees extending on to the lagoon, as can be seen in the background of the 1843 lithograph below.

Giussepe Valeriani drew the Redentore as he saw it in 1719 when he first arrived in Venice, and one hundred years later Turner sketched San Giorgio with the Redentore behind it. The facade of San Giorgio was completed by Vincenzo Scamozzi (1552-1616) between 1597 and 1610. Andrea Palladio's (1518-1580) original designs called for the pillars and pilasters to begin at the same level, as in the facade of Redentore. The pillars and pilasters of his other church facade—that of San Francesco degla Vigna (p. 120)—also have a uniform base but are raised off the ground by a plinth. Scamozzi appears to have combined these two features with a not altogether happy result.

enquiry, was peculiarly capable of being used as an indirect stimulus to moods of devotion and contrition. Next to the finest mosaics of the first centuries, the early works of Giovanni Bellini, the greatest Venetian master of the 15th century, best fulfil this religious intention. Painting has in his life-time reached a point where the difficulties of technique no longer stood in the way of the expression of profound emotion. No one can look at Bellini's pictures of the Dead Christ upheld by the Virgin or angels without being put into a mood of deep contrition, nor at his earlier Madonnas without a thrill of awe and reverence. And Giovanni Bellini does not stand alone. His contemporaries Gentile Bellini, the Vivarini, Crivelli, and Cima da Conegliano all began by painting in the same spirit, and produced almost the same effect.

Berenson.

Marino Faliero became Doge in 1354 when his age was seventy-six, having been both a soldier and a diplomatist. He found himself at once involved in the war with Genoa, and almost immediately came the battle of Sapienza, when the Genoese took five thousand prisoners, including the admiral, Niccoló Pisani. This blow was a very serious one for the Venetians, involving as it did great loss of life, and there was a growing feeling that they were badly governed. The Doge, who was but a figure-head of the Council of Ten, secretly thinking so too, plotted for the overthrow of the Council and the establishment of himself in supreme power. The Arsenal men were to form his chief army in the revolt; the false alarm of a Genoese attack was to get the populace together; and then the blow was to be struck and Faliero proclaimed prince. But the plot miscarried through one of the conspirators warning a friend to keep indoors; the ringleaders were caught and hanged or exiled; and the Doge, after confessing his guilt, was beheaded in the courtyard of his palace. . . . Of his unhappy story Byron made a drama.

One of Faliero's party was Calendario, an architect, employed on the part of the Doge's Palace in which we are now standing. He was hanged or strangled between the two red columns in the upper arches of the Piazzetta façade. . . .

Before leaving the Hall one should, as I have said, walk to the balcony, the door of which the custodian opens for each visitor with a mercenary hand. It should of course be free to all; and Venice would do well to appoint some official (if such could be found) to enforce such liberties. Immediately below is all the movement of the Molo; then the edge of the lagoon with its myriad gondolas; then the sparkling water, with all its busy activities and swaying gondoliers; and away beyond it the lovely island of S. Giorgio. A fairer prospect the earth cannot show.

Lucas.

The route leads finally to the prisons.

About the air and light condition and the inhuman treatment meeted out to the prisoners in the *Pozzi*, many exaggerated accounts have been repeated especially by the democratic revolutionaries in 1797, or reported by not very scrupulous historians and writers, which resulted in exaggerated ideas of the terrifying and cruel methods of government of the ancient Republic. The Venetian administration, on the contrary, did not adopt more cruel methods than the other governments when all conditions and usages in those days are taken into account; indeed, it tried to alleviate the prisoners' lot with more humane treatment and with special improvements, and also by stimulating public charity. The 18 vaulted cells, built with blocks of Istrian stone, receive indirect light from the passage; they are divided into two rows and were covered with thick boards of wood; boards too served as beds; only one cell is today kept in its original state. Each cell used to have a special name (Galeotta, Vulcana, Moceniga, Leona), or was named with a Roman numeral upside down; on the walls, names, sentences and rough drawings, mostly of the C16, can still be seen.

Lorenzetti.

I descended from the cheerful day into two ranges, one below another, of dismal, awful, horrible stone cells. They were quite dark. Each had a loophole in its massive walls, where, in the old time, every day a torch was placed, to light the prisoners within, for half an hour. The captives, by the glimmering of these brief rays, had cut and scratched inscriptions in the blackened vaults. I saw them. For their labour with the rusty nail's point had outlived their agony and them through many generations.

One cell I saw, in which no man remained for more than four-and-twenty hours, long marked for dead before he entered it. Hard by another, a dismal one, whereto, at midnight, the confessor came—a monk, brown-robed and hooded—ghastly in the day and free bright air, but in the midnight of the murky prison, Hope's extinguisher and Murder's herald. I had my foot upon the spot where, at the same dread hour, the shriven prisoner was strangled; and struck my hand upon the guilty door—low-browed and stealthy—through which the lumpish sack was carried out into a boat and rowed away, and drowned where it was death to cast a net.

Dickens.

The Council of Ten, which had a hand in everything, which disposed without appeal of life and death, of financial affairs and military appointments, which included the Inquisitors among its number, and which over-threw Foscari, as it had overthrown so many powerful men before—this Council was yearly chosen afresh from the whole governing body, the Gran Consilio, and consequently was the most direct expression of its will. It is not probable that serious intrigues occurred at these elections, as the short duration of the office and the accountability which followed rendered it an object of no great desire. But violent and mysterious as the proceedings of this and other authorities might be, the genuine Venetian conoted rather than fled their sentence, not only because the Republic had long arms, and if it could not catch him, might punish his family, but because in most cases it acted from national motives, and not from a thirst for blood. No State has ever exercised a greater moral influence over its subjects, whether abroad or at home. Every Venetian away from home was a born spy for his Government. It was a matter of course that the Venetian Cardinals at Rome sent home news of the transactions of secret Papal Consistories. Cardinal D. Grimani had the dispatches intercepted in the neighbourhood of Rome (1500) which Ascanio Sforza was sending to his brother Ludovico il Moro, and forwarded them to Venice; his father at that time exposed to a serious accusation, claimed public credit for this service of his son before the Gran Consilio.

Burckhardt.

Come out of the courtyard of the Ducal Palace; the island of San Giorgio faces us across the lagoon. It can be reached by gondola, or much more economically by vaporetto (just beyond the Danieli).

Most of the area of the island is now occupied by the Cini Foundation —a cultural foundation—which has recently restored and extended the C16 and C17 monastery buildings. The entrance is on the right when you land. The cloisters and beyond them the new buildings and garden (including an open-air theatre) stretching to the Lagoon on the far side of the island are of immense charm. If you do not have permission to visit the Foundation, you can return and see these by attending one of the concerts or other manifestations which take place here from time to time. The photographs in the bar give a vivid impression of the neglect and desecration which the buildings suffered when they were occupied by the army. But admission to a concert does not theoretically give access to the most distinguished structures—the staircase and the most elegant library—both by Longhena.

The staircase is on the right in the cloisters which go straight ahead from the entrance.

In the staircase hall of the monastery of S. Giorgio Maggiore (1643/5) where two parallel flights ascend along the walls to a common landing. Longhena once again proved his consummate skill as a master of scenic architecture. This staircase hall is far in advance of its time; it has made a deep impression on architects, particularly in Northern Italy, and was taken up and developed in countries north of the Alps.

Wittokower.

The Library (1641) is reached from the top of the stairs, along the corridor to the opposite side of the building.

The late C16 church of San Giorgio Maggiore is one of Palladio's most distinguished works. On the walls of the church are two pictures, both best seen from the altar rail. On the left wall: Tintoretto: *The Fall of Manna.*

One of Tintoret's most remarkable landscapes. Another painter would have made the congregation hurrying to gather the manna, and wondering at it. Tintoret at once makes us remember that they have been fed with it 'by space of forty years.'

Ruskin.

On the right wall: Tintoretto: *The Last Supper.*

It was the whole scene that Tintoret seemed to have beheld in a flash of inspiration intense enough to stamp it ineffaceably on his perception: and it was the whole scene, complete, peculiar, individual, unprecedented, that he committed to canvas with all the vehemence of his talent. Compare his 'Last Supper' at San Giorgio—its long, diagonally placed table, its dusky spaciousness, its scattered lamp-light and halo-light, its startled gesticulating figures, its richly realistic foreground—with the customary formal, almost mathematical rendering of the subject, in which impressiveness seems to have been sought in elimination rather than comprehension. You get from Tintoret's work the impression that he felt, pictorially, the great, beautiful, terrible spectacle of human life very much as Shakespeare felt it poetically—with a heart that never ceased to beat a passionate accompaniment to every stroke of his brush.

Henry James.

In the Last Supper of S. Giorgio, one of his latest works, the extent of Tintoretto's deviation from Renaissance precepts may be readily measured by comparing it with the classic example of that time—Leonardo's. In Tintoretto's picture the viewpoint is very high—we are looking down on the room from above the heads of the figures—and the recession of the table is odd and irrational in its violent asymmetry in the picture space. Of the individual figures it may be noted that the servant in the right foreground, seen from the back balanced on one foot and making an affected gesture with his left hand while turning to the kneeling woman, would not be out of place in any Central Italian Mannerist composition. He in fact constitutes the main formal balance to the violent perspective of the table. But we only notice him late, if at all; (both here and in the Agony* the faces of nearly all the figures are either averted or in shadow: this principle is fundamental to Tintoretto's art). Our eyes are directed to Christ with His own mysterious light, to the fiercely burning lamp (perhaps symbolizing the Holy Spirit) and to the ghostly cherubim who sweep down through the ceiling.

Gould.

The C16 Choir stalls show scenes from the life of Saint Benedict. On the left is the entrance to the Sacristy (across passage), with C17 panelling and an attractive clock on the wall. The arrow points to the lift for the campanile: from the top, a fine view of the town and lagoon more varied and interesting than the view from the campanile in the Piazza. (It merits a further visit at sunset.)

The two great constituents of the Venetian landscape, the sea and the sky, are precisely the two features in \Nature which undergo the most incessant change. The cloud-wreaths of this evening's sunset will never be repeated again; the bold and buttressed piles of those cloud-mountains will never be built again just so for us; the grain of orange and crimson that stains the water before our prow, we cannot be sure that we shall look upon its like again. The revolutions of the seasons will, no doubt, repeat certain effects: spring will chill the waters to a cold, hard green; summer will spread its breadth of golden light on palace front and waterway; autumn will come with its pearly grey sirocco days, and sunsets flaming with a myriad hues; the stars of a cloudless winter night, the whole vast dome of heaven, will be reflected in the mirrors of the still lagoon. But in spite of this general order of the seasons, one day is less like another day in Venice than anywhere else; the lagoon wears a different aspect each morning when you rise, the sky offers a varied composition of cloud each evening as the sun sets.

Horatio F. Brown.

* In the Scuola San Rocco, p. 166.

Once did she hold the gorgeous East in fee,
And was the safeguard of the West: the worth
Of Venice did not fall below her birth,
Venice, the eldest child of liberty.
She was a maiden city, bright and free;
No guile seduced, no force could violate;
And when she took unto herself a mate,
She must espouse the everlasting sea.
And what if she had seen those glories fade,
Those titles vanish, and that strength decay,
Yet shall some tribute of regret be paid
When her long life hath reached its final day:
Men are we, and must grieve when even the shade
Of that which once was great has passed away.

Wordsworth.

2

Correr Piture Gallery – Santa Maria della Salute Accademia

The entrance to the Correr Museum is under the colonnades at the end of the Piazza opposite to San Marco—in the Ala Napoleonica. In Room 4, a number of stone fragments: on the left of the exit door a lion's mouth, used for secret accusations against tax evaders.

Room 6

Heinz: *Festa Del Redentore*, showing the bridge of boats over to the Redentore church, on the Giudecca. The ceremony is still observed, on the third Sunday in July.

In Heinz: *A Ducal Audience*, can be seen the very high shoes, the *baute*, worn by women in the C17.

> While Italian art again and again lifts its subjects outside time, Northern artists more usually emphasize the moment of actuality, a room cluttered with everyday objects, a window giving upon an almost unnaturally clear landscape or townscape—as if embalmed in a glass paperweight. This interest in immediacy was to be the impetus behind Venetian view painting. The first painters of the city for its own sake were in fact Northern artists, with their uncomplicated ability for painting what their eyes fell upon.
>
> Heinz seems to have reached Venice by 1625; a contemporary described him in 1660 as 'l'piu capricioso', and the adjective will serve for the lively doll-like figures who cram his pictures.
>
> *Levey.*

The picture gallery (*Quadreria*) is at the far end and upstairs. The mounting of the pictures is striking, if a little self-conscious; but they are all clean, well hung and remarkably well lit.

The following merit special attention:

Room 10

Breughel: *Adoration of the Magi.*

Room 11
    Bouts: *Madonna and Child.*
    da Messina: *Pietà.*

Room 12
    Bruyn: *Portrait of a Woman.*

Room 13
    Jacopo Bellini: *Crucifixion.*
    Giovanni Bellini: *Madonna and Child.*
    Giovanni Bellini: *Pietà.*
    Giovanni Bellini: *Transfiguration.*
    Giovanni Bellini: *Doge Giovanni Mocenigo.*
    Giovanni Bellini: *Crucifixion.*

When one goes into the Renaissance galleries, it is as if one suddenly realized that in all the others one had been suffering from a blurred short-sightedness. And this is not because many of the paintings have been finely cleaned, nor because chiaroscuro was a later convention. It is because every Flemish and Italian Renaissance artist believed that it was his subject itself—not his way of painting it—which had to express the emotions and ideas he intended. . . . It is this difference—the difference between the pictures being a starting-off point and a destination—that explains the clarity, the visual definitiveness, the tactile values of Renaissance art. The Renaissance painter limited himself to an exclusive concern with what the spectator could see, as opposed to what he might infer. . . .

This attitude had several important results. It forbade any attempt at literal naturalism because the only appeal of naturalism is the inference that it is 'just life like': it obviously isn't, in fact, like life because the picture is only a static image. It prevented all merely subjective suggestibility. It forced the artist, as far as his knowledge allowed him, to deal simultaneously with all the visual aspects of his subject—colour, light, mass, line, movement, structure, and not, as has increasingly happened since, to concentrate only on one aspect and to infer the others. It allowed him to combine more richly than any later artists have done realism and decoration, observation and formalization. The idea that they are incompatible is only based on today's assumption that their inferences are incompatible; visually an embroidered surface or drapery, invented as the most beautiful mobile architecture ever, can combine with realistic anatomical analysis as naturally as the courtly and physical combine in Shakespeare.

But above all, the Renaissance artist's attitude made him use

to its maximum the most expressive visual form in the world—
the human body. Later the nude became an idea—Arcadia or
Bohemia. But during the Renaissance every eyelid, breast, wrist,
baby's foot, nostril, was a double celebration of fact: the fact of
the miraculous structure of the human body and the fact that only
through the senses of this body can we apprehend the rest of the
visible, tangible world.

This lack of ambiguity is the Renaissance, and its superb
combination of sensuousness and nobility stemmed from a
confidence which cannot be artificially re-created. But when we
eventually achieve a confident society again, its art may well have
more to do with the Renaissance than with any of the moral or
political artistic theories of the nineteenth century. Meanwhile,
it is a salutary reminder for us even today that, as Berenson has
said so often and so wisely, the vitality of European art lies in its
'tactile values and movement' which are the result of the observation of the 'corporal significance of objects'.

Berger.

Giovanni Bellini, often called 'Giambellino', studied for a long
time while with his father. Then, continuing in the vigorous
manner of his brother-in-law, Mantegna, he sought to discover a
fresh approach to atmosphere and tonality in which light was to
determine spatial organization. During a trip to the mainland in
1473, Giovanni probably came to know the art of Piero della
Francesca. He was marked by the painting of Antonello da
Messina who worked in Venice in 1475. These two contacts
were of decisive influence on his development. With Giovanni
Bellini, Venetian painting reached the maturity which made
possible the later innovations of Giorgione.

Bellini's earliest known works . . . are still very Mantegna-like
in feeling, but the outlines are already more pliant and the lighting
subtler. In the *Crucifixion* of the Correr museum, the Virgin and
Saint John still bear the mark of the Paduan painter's influence,
but the vast landscape with its quiet river and golden horizon
reveals a personal sense of luminous space. Giambellino gives
increasing importance to the skies in his compositions and to the
special quality of the atmosphere.

Chastel.

Room 14
Alvise Vivarini: *Saint Anthony of Padua.*
Compare with the figure in his *Sacred Conversation*—Accademia
Gallery, Room XXII (p. 105).

Room 15

Carpaccio: *Two Venetian Ladies*. The child and the dog are cut off by the left-hand edge: the picture was formerly bigger. The roof terraces (*altane*) are thought to provide an explanation for the 'golden tresses' of Venetian painting: the hair, wet with a chemical solution and spread over the brim of a crownless hat bleached in the sun while giving shade to its owner.

I know . . . no other which unites every nameable quality of painter's art in so intense a degree—breadth with tenderness, brilliancy with quietness, decision with minuteness, colour with light and shade: all that is faithfullest in Holland, fancifullest in Venice, severest in Florence, naturalest in England. Whatever de Hooghe could do in shade, Van Eyck in detail, Giorgione in mass, Titian in colour, Bewick and Landseer in animal life, is here at once; and I know no other picture in the world which can be compared with it.

Ruskin.

It has been named 'The Two Courtesans', largely because of the daringly décolleté dresses. But these were in fact quite normal for bourgeois women in the 1490s, and the very high shoes are of a type worn only by the respectably married—'those pattens must make it difficult for your wife to walk' remarked a traveller to a Venetian: 'so much the better' was the reply.

Honour.

The growing delight in life with the consequent love of health, beauty, and joy were felt more powerfully in Venice than anywhere else in Italy. The explanation of this may be found in the character of the Venetian government which was such that it gave little room for the satisfaction of the passion for personal glory, and kept its citizens so busy in duties of state that they had small leisure for learning. Some of the chief passions of the Renaissance thus finding no outlet in Venice, the other passions insisted all the more on being satisfied. Venice, moreover, was the only state in Italy which was enjoying, and for many generations had been enjoying, internal peace. This gave the Venetians a love of comfort, of ease and of splendour, a refinement of manner, and humaneness of feeling, which made them the first really modern people in Europe.

Thus it came to pass that in the Venetian pictures of the end of the fifteenth century we find neither the contrition nor the devotion of those earlier years when the Church alone employed painting as the interpreter of emotion, nor the learning which characterised the Florentines. The Venetian masters of this time, although nominally continuing to paint the Madonna and saints, were in reality painting handsome, healthy, sane people like themselves, people who wore their splendid robes with dignity, who found life worth the mere living and sought no metaphysical basis for it.

The Church itself had educated its children to understanding painting as a language. Now that the passions men dared to avow were no longer connected with happiness in some future state only, but mainly with life in the present, painting was expected to give voice to these more human aspirations and to desert the outgrown ideals of the Church.

Berenson.

Room 16
Carpaccio: *Man in a Red Hat.*

Room 17
Lotto: *Madonna and Child Crowned with Angels.*
(See also Riccio's bust in this room.)

Out of the museum in the opposite direction from the Piazza; slightly to the left, into the Calle dell'Ascensione; first on left, down the Calle Vallaresso, to the gondola ferry (*traghetto*), Immediately across the canal is the customs house (*Dogana*).

The statue of Fortune, forming the weathercock, standing on the world, is alike characteristic of the conceits of the time and of the hopes and principles of the last days of Venice.

Ruskin.

The charming architectural promontory of the Dogana stretches out the most graceful arms, balancing in its hand the gilded globe on which revolves the delightful satirical figure of a little weathercock of a woman. This Fortune, this Navigation, or whatever she is called—she surely needs no name—catches the wind in the bit of drapery of which she has divested her rotary bronze loveliness. On the other side of the Canal twinkles and glitters the long row of the happy palaces which are mainly expensive hotels. There is a little of everything everywhere, in the bright Venetian air, but to these houses belongs especially the appearance of sitting, across the water, at the receipt of custom, of watching in their hypocritical loveliness for the stranger and the victim. I call them happy, because even their sordid uses and their vulgar signs melt somehow, with their vague sea-stained pinks and drabs, into that strange gaiety of light and colour which is made up of the reflection of superannuated things. The atmosphere plays over them like a laugh, they are of the essence

of places as they are from their own balconies, and share fully in that universal privilege of Venetian objects which consists of being both the picture and the point of view.

Henry James.

Some way to the right of the Dogana is the church of Santa Maria della Salute—'of health' because it was built to celebrate the end of a plague in the C17. The wall on the left before the Church contains the entrance to the Venice Seminary, a C17 building now housing Manfredinian Picture Gallery—a collection of sculpture and pictures. Only the very energetic should attempt to include this collection; for other readers I suggest a few moments sitting on the steps which lead down to the Canal from the Salute—a good spot to read the following.

Venice is nowadays unthinkable without the picturesque silhouette of the church, which dominates the entrance to the Canal Grande; but it would be wrong to insist too much on the picturesqueness of the building, as is usually done, while forgetting that this is in every respect one of the most interesting and subtle structures of the entire 17th century. . . . The salient feature of the plan is a regular octagon surrounded by an ambulatory. . . . The **elevation . . . is a free adaptation of a well-known North Italian** type derived from Bramante, Santa Maria della Salute differing from the Renaissance models mainly in the decorative interpretation of the columns. Instead of continuing the columns of the octagon into the architecture of the drum, we find a large figure topping the projecting entablature of each column. It is these iconographically important figures of prophets that turn each **column into an isolated unit and at the same time emphasise the** enclosed centralised character of the main room. . . .

From Palladio derives the colouristic treatment: grey stone for the structural parts and whitewash for the walls and fillings. But **it should be remembered that this was not Palladio's speciality:** it had, in fact, a mediaeval pedigree, was taken up and systemised by Brunelleschi, and after him used by most architects who were connected with the classical Florentine tradition. The architects **of the Roman Baroque never employed this method of differentia-tion, the isolating effect of which would have interfered with the dynamic rhythms of their buildings. In contrast, however, to** Florentine procedure, where colour invariably sustains a coherent metrical system, Longhena's colour scheme is not logical; colour for him was an optical device which enabled him to support or suppress elements of the composition, thereby directing the beholder's vision.

Many details of the Salute are also Palladian, such as the orders, the columns placed on high pedestals (see S. Giorgio Maggiore)

The upper illustration is of the Procuratoire Nuove from the *Gran Teatro di Venezia*. It was begun by Scamozzi in 1586 as an echo of Sansovino's library and completed (gracefully altered) when Longhena refined the work in 1640. This engraving by Antonio Vissentini (1688-1782) of the Piazza from Canaletto's drawing of 1754 shows the church of San Geminiano in the centre background. This building was pulled down by the French to complete the arcade, and to create in Napoleon's words 'the best drawing room in Europe'.

On October 3, 1786 Goethe sketched the lawyer Reccaini and wrote 'In the Ducal Palace I witnessed an important trial. One of the advocates was everything an exaggerated *buffo* should be: short and fat but agile, a very prominent profile, a booming voice and an impassioned eloquence as though everything he said came from the bottom of his heart'.

and the segmental windows with mullions in the chapels, the type derived from Roman thermae and introduced by Palladio into ecclesiastical architecture (S. Giorgió, Il Redentore). All these elements combine to give the Salute the severe and chaste appearance of a Palladian structure, but it can be shown that Palladio's influence was even more vital.

One of Longhena's chief problems consisted in preserving the octagonal form outside without sacrificing clarity and lucidity inside. By the seemingly simple device of making the sides of two consecutive pillars parallel to each other he succeeded in giving the optically important units of the ambulatory and the chapels regular geometrical shapes, entirely in the spirit of the Renaissance. The full meaning of this organisation is revealed only when one stands in the ideal and real centre of the octagon. Looking from this point in any direction, the spectator will find that entirely homogeneous 'pictures' always appear in the field of vision. Longhena's passionate interest in determining the holder's field of vision is surely one of the factors which made him choose the problematical octagon with ambulatory instead of one of the traditional Renaissance designs over a centralised plan. It cannot be emphasised too strongly that no other type of plan allows only carefully integrated views to be seen; here the eye is not given a chance to wander off and make conquests of its own.

It would seem that the centralisation of the octagon could not have been carried any further. Moreover, the sanctuary which is reached over a few steps, appears only loosely connected with the octagon. Following the North Italian Renaissance tradition of centralised plans (Bramante's Santa Maria di Canepànova), main room and sanctuary form almost independent units. For the two large apses of the domed sanctuary Longhena employed a system entirely different from that of the octagon; he used giant pilasters instead of columns and replaced the mullioned windows of the chapel by normal windows in two tiers. . . .

A third room, the rectangular choir, is separated from the sanctuary by an arch resting on pairs of free-standing columns, between which the view is blocked by the large High Altar. Inside the choir the architecture changes again: two small orders of pilasters are placed one above the other. At the far end of the choir three small arches appear in the field of vision.

From the entrance of the church the columns and the arch framing the High Altar lie in the field of vision—it is important that only this motif and no more is visible—and the beholder is directed to the spiritual centre of the church through a sequence of arches, one behind the other: from the octagon to the ambulatory and the altar and, concluding the vista, to the arched wall of the choir. Thus, in spite of the Renaissance-like isolation of spatial entities and in spite of the carefully calculated centralisation of the octagon, there is a scenic progression along the longitudinal axis. . . .

In Santa Maria della Salute scenery appears behind scenery like wings on the stage. Instead of inviting the eye—as the Roman Baroque architects did—to glide along the walls and savour a spatial continuum, Longhena constantly determines the vistas across the spaces. . . .

Like the interior, the picturesque exterior of Santa Maria della Salute was the result of sober deliberation. The thrust of the large dome is diverted onto pairs of buttresses (the Scrolls) which rest on the arches of the ambulatory. The side walls of the chapels (aligned with these arches) are therefore buttments to the dome. . . .

The large dome of the Salute has an inner and outer vault, the outer one consisting of lead over wood, in keeping with the Venetian custom (including Palladio). While the principal dome ultimately derives from that of St. Peter's, the subsidiary dome with its stilted form over a simple circular brick drum and framed by two campanili follows the Byzantine-Venetian tradition. The grouping together of a main and subsidiary dome fits well into the Venetian *ambiente*—the domes of S. Marco are quite near—but never before has the silhouette been so boldly enriched by the use of entirely different types of domes and drums in one and the same building. No less important than the aspect of the domes from a distance is the near view of the lower zone from the Canal Grande. From here the chapels right and left of the main entrance are conspicuous. They are therefore elaborately treated like little church façades in their own right. . . . Their small order is taken up in the gigantic triumphal arch motif in the main entrance. It is this motif that sets the seal on the entire composition.

The central arch with the framing columns corresponds exactly to the interior arches of the octagon, so that the theme is given before one enters the church. In addition the small order also repeats that inside, and the niches for statues in two tiers conform to the windows in the sanctuary. And more than this: the façade is, in fact, devised like a *scenae frons,* and with the central door thrown wide open, as shown in a contemporary engraving, the consequitive sequence of arches inside the church contained by the triumphal arch, conjures up a proper stage setting.

Wittkower.

Inside the church, first altar on right—Giordano: *Presentation of the Virgin.*

The great building of seventeenth century Venice—the sole great artistic feat of the city in that century—was Longhena's

S. Maria della Salute; and it is hardly an exaggeration to say that this church with its air-borne domes and sea-washed steps needed merely to be brushed on to the canvasses of Canaletto and Guardi to become rococo.

Rococo before its time, it was suitably decorated by a non-Venetian painter, rococo also before the time, Luca Giordano (1632–1705). He left three altarpieces in the church, of which the *Presentation of the Virgin* with its elaborate architectural setting and its radiant shafts of light preludes the new style and also provides a welcome piece of grand decoration amid the gloomy darkness of seventeenth century Venetian art. Despite its grimy appearance today, the picture is really painted with startlingly bright cool colours: there is generous use of white and a strong blue juxtaposed to it—very much as Tiepolo was to juxtapose them half a century later in the Palazzo Labia frescoes. The commission for these altar pieces was given to Giordano in 1685 and reveals that the visiting artist was preferred for this important work to any native talent available at the time. Giordano's legacy to Venice did not go unperceived, it seems, and a few years later the style of his altarpieces was no longer an isolated phenomenon but, made more graceful and less rigorous, had become a Venetian style.

Levey.

In the Sacristy (entrance slightly to left of High Altar): wall over altar—Titian: *Five Saints.* Altar front—dirty C15 tapestry: *Descent of Holy Ghost.* Wall opposite entrance—Tintoretto: *Marriage at Cana.*

. . . one is surprised to find Tintoret whose tone of mind was always grave, and who did not like to make a picture out of brocades and diadems, throwing his whole strength into the conception of a marriage feast; but so it is, and there are assuredly no female heads in any of his pictures in Venice elaborated so far as those which here form the central light. Neither is it often that the works of this mighty master conform themselves to any of the rules acted upon by ordinary painters; but in this instance the popular laws have been observed, and an academy student would be delighted to see with what severity the principal light is arranged in a central mass, which is divided and made more brilliant by a vigorous piece of shadow thrust into the midst of it, and which dies away in lesser fragments and sparkling towards the extremities of the picture. This mass of light is as interesting by its composition as by its intensity. The cicerone who escorts the stranger round the sacristy in the course of five minutes, which allows him some forty seconds for the contemplation of a picture, which the study of six months would not entirely fathom, directs his attention very carefully to the 'bell' effetto di prospettivo', the whole merit of the picture being, in the eyes of the intelligent public, that there is a long table in it, one end of which looks farther off than the other; but there is more in the 'bell' effetto di prospettivo' than the observance of the common law of optics. The table is set in a spacious chamber, of which the windows at the end let in the light from the horizon, and those in the side wall the intense blue of an Eastern sky. The spectator looks all along the table, at the farther end of which are seated Christ, and the Madonna, the marriage guests on each side of it—on one side men, on the other women; the men are set with their backs to the light, which passing over their heads and glancing slightly on the tablecloth, falls in full length along the line of young Venetian women, who thus fill the whole centre of the picture with one broad sunbeam, made up of fair faces and golden hair. Close to the spectator a woman has risen in amazement, and stretches across the table to show the wine in her cup to those opposite; her dark red dress intercepts **and enhances the mass of gathered light. It is rather curious,** considering the subject of the picture, that one cannot distinguish either the bride or bridegroom; but the fourth figure from the Madonna in the line of women, who wears a white head-dress of lace and rich chains of pearls in her hair, may well be accepted for the former, and I think that between her and the woman on the Madonna's left hand the unity of the line of women is intercepted by a male figure. The tone of the whole picture is sober and majestic in the highest degree; the dresses are all broad masses of colour, and the only parts of the picture which lay claim to the expression of wealth or splendour are the head-dresses of the women. In this respect the conception of the scene differs widely from that of Veronese, and approaches more nearly to the probable truth. Still the marriage is not an unimportant one; an immense crowd, filling the background, forming a superbly rich mosaic of colour against the distant sky. Taken as a whole, the picture is perhaps the most perfect example which human art has produced of the utmost possible force and sharpness of shadow united with richness of local colour. This picture unites colour as rich as Titian's with light and shade as forcible as Rembrandt's, and far **more decisive.**

Ruskin.

Same wall—St. Sebastian, attributed to Basaiti. On walls—three panels by Titian: *The Sacrifice of Abraham, David Killing Goliath, Cain and Abel.*

Outside the church, left over Ponte dell'Abbazia di San Gregorio, under arch. At number 172, on right door to C14 cloisters of Abbazia di S. Gregorio. Ring bell for visit (private property). Fine view of pool of St. Mark's.

> The loveliest cortile I know in Venice.
>
> *Ruskin.*

We go on, via Campo San Gregorio and Calle San Gregorio (glass blowing at No. 175b) and Calle San Cristoforo (the entrance to the Guggenheim Collection may be noted for future reference) to Campo San Vio. Immediately to the right on entering we see the English Church.

> ..For a taste of Venetian Englishry, go on a summer morning to the Anglican Church of St. George, which is a converted warehouse near the Accademia bridge. Its pews are usually full, and the familiar melodies of Ancient and Modern stream away, turgid but enthusiastic, across the Grand Canal. The drone of the visiting padre blends easily with the hot buzz of the Venetian summer, and when the service ends you will see his surplice fluttering in the doorway, among the neat hats and tweedy suits, the white gloves and prayer-books, the scrubbed children and the pink-cheeked, tight-curled, lavender-scented, pearl-necklaced, regimentally brooched ladies that so admirably represent year in, year out, east and west, the perennial spirit of England abroad.
>
> Nowadays they are only summer visitors, and in winter the little church is closed, and looks neglected and forgotten. Once, though, it was the flourishing chapel of the permanent Anglo-American community in Venice, in the days when there was such a thing. Around its walls are elegant epitaphs to forgotten English gentlewomen, often titled and usually the daughters of gallant officers; and sometimes you will find upon your seat a curiously anachronistic appeal for funds, which was evidently overprinted when it first appeared half a century ago, and is still faithfully distributed—although the chaplain, the British and American Hospital and the Seamen's Institute for which it appeals have all long since disappeared.
>
> *Morris.*

It is worth going down to the water for the view across the Canal, and especially for the view of the large Palazzo Corner della Ca'Grande built in the C16 from a project by Sansovino.

> The classical elements, rusticated on the ground floor, Ionic and Corinthian on the first and second, are adapted to the constructional character of the city and to the traditional Venetian house in which the windows and ample terraces in the forms of

loggias acquire fundamental importance in the architectural mass because of the prevalence of empty spaces over solid ones.

Lorenzetti.

From the far end of the Campo, we go along the Fondamenta di Ca'Bregadin, and emerge facing the Giudecca Island across the water. Turn right over the bridge and along the Fondamenta delle Zattere to the church of the Gesuati.

On the ceiling
Three fine frescoes by G. B. Tiepolo.

Left Side, First Chapel
G. B. Tiepolo: *Virgin and Saints.*

Left Side, Third Chapel
Piazzetta: *Three Saints.*

> While colour was brightening even garishly the rococo painter's canvases, Piazzetta was restricting his palette to chestnut, black white and grey. Working within that deliberately narrow range, his genius achieved at least one great tonal coup in *Saints Vincent Hyacinth and Lorenzo Bertrando* for the new Dominican church, the Gesuati: an altarpiece which is probably the greatest picture of its kind set up in Venice in the 18th century. He simply disposes his three saints in a cloudy nondescript atmosphere and from their juxtaposed habits of black, white and grey, he makes more effective contrast than would another painter with a whole rainbow of colours. Unlike the majority of his contemporaries he aims at tonal effects, gradations and harmonies of monochrome, and he cuts down the amount of light in the picture in a manner almost rebuking the superb chromatic brilliance of Tiepolo's ceiling in the same church, also painted in 1739.
>
> The taste for reproducing the trivia of life which runs in Venice from the history painters, to the view painters, via genre, is absent from Piazzetta. The clothes of his people have a simplicity that is sculptural; and his concentration on the figure, like his subdued unified tonality, is sculptural too. Perhaps there is really some genuine relevance in the fact that his father had been a sculptor or a wood-carver; perhaps from him Piazzetta inherited that feeling for the monumental that makes him stand out so boldly and forcefully amid the gentle coloured mists of most 18th century Venetian art.

Levey.

Right Side (i.e. last before exit)
Sebastiano Ricci: *Pius V and Saints.*

Outside the church, it is worth going a few yards to the right to see the 'Lion's Mouth' let into the wall at No. 1919. Like the others, it was used for anonymous accusations—in this case concerning the sanitary department.

Turn about now and take—on the left immediately after the Gesuati church—the Rio Terrá Foscarini to the Accademia Bridge. On the entrance door of the Accademy (beyond the foot of the bridge) are displayed the opening times. Allow at least two hours for the Gallery: even the selection given below runs to 93 pictures. If there is time, have coffee now at the foot of the bridge—in summer, under the umbrellas beside the canal.

> As late as 1848 the Austrian soldiers could prevent subversive foot passage across the city simply by closing the Rialto bridge. Then two iron structures were thrown across the water-way—one by the railway station, one near the Accademia gallery. They were flat, heavy, and very ugly, and the Accademia bridge was sometimes known, in mixed irony and affection, as *Ponte Inglese*. Both lasted until the 1930s, when they had to be replaced because of the increased size of the 'vaporetti'. The new station bridge was a handsome stone structure, far higher than the Rialto. The new Accademia bridge was of precisely the same proportions, but because money was short it was built (just for the time being, so they cheerfully said) of tarred wood—a return to the original materials of Venetian bridge building.
>
> *Morris.*

My tendency to look at the world through the eyes of the painter whose pictures I have seen last has given me an odd idea. Since our eyes are educated from childhood on by the objects we see around us, a Venetian painter is bound to see the world as a brighter and gayer place than most people see it. We northerners who spend our lives in a drab and, because of the dirt and dust, an uglier country where even reflected light is subdued, and who have, most of us, to live in cramped rooms—we cannot instinctively develop an eye which looks with such delight at the world.

As I glided over the lagoons in the brilliant sunshine and saw the gondoliers in their colourful costume, gracefully poised against the blue sky as they rowed with easy strokes across the light-green surface of the water, I felt I was looking at the latest and best painting of the Venetian school. The sunshine raised the local colours to a dazzling glare and even the parts in shadow were so light that they could have served pretty well as sources of light. The same could be said of the reflections in the water. Everything was painted clearly on a clear background. It only needed the sparkle of a white-crested wave to put the dot on the i.

Goethe.

Accademia

Room I, facing entrance

No. 21: Paolo Veneziano: *Coronation of the Virgin.*

The first name to appear in the history of Venetian painting is that of Paolo Veneziano, who worked between 1321 and 1360. His manner is closely related to the Byzantine art of the period, with which he may have become familiar during a visit to Constantinople, or simply through the numerous mosaics, icons and miniatures in Venice. However he gradually acquired a more supple style, closer to the elegance of the Italian Trecento.

At the time he was painting the *Coronation of the Virgin* (ca. 1345) he was still wavering between these two forms of expression. The motifs in the *Coronation of the Virgin* derive from the 13th century Greek miniatures, the figures of Saints have the same delicacy, the gold-embroidered gowns and Santa Clara's striped cloak are of Oriental fabrics. But iconographic details, such as the Virgin's crown and the angels holding the draperies behind the central group, belong to the Gothic tradition. The sharper brush-strokes and the freer arrangement of draperies further indicate a development that culminated in his late works: the *Madonna* in the Louvre (1353) and the *Coronation of the Virgin* in the Frick Collection (1358).

Thus even though he remained unaware of Giotto's decisive contribution, Paolo Veneziano's art bears the mark of Western elegance. By remaining faithful to the bright colours and gold ornamentation of Byzantine splendour, Paolo determined the precious, decorative manner of late 14th century art.

Chastel.

Room II

No. 36: Giovanni Bellini: *Madonna and Saints.*
No. 166: Giovanni Bellini: *Mourning for Jesus.*
No. 611: Cima da Conegliano: *St. Thomas.*
No. 44: Carpaccio: *Presentation of Jesus in the Temple.*
No. 815: Cima da Conegliano: *Madonna of the Orange-Tree.*
No. 39: Marco Basaiti: *Calling of the Sons of Zebedee.*
No. 38: Giovanni Bellini: *Madonna and Saints.*
No. 69: Marco Basaiti: *Agony in the Garden.*

Its inspiration is obviously Bellinesque, and although the theme derives from the Bellini of half a century earlier, the breadth of the handling owes something to later works of the master. The glow of the sky round the figure of Christ is altogether in the spirit of Bellini, but the conception of the scene—as of a proscenium arch with the curtain up and the four saints standing like a chorus outside it—strikes, in an easel picture, a somewhat artificial and un-Bellinesque note. At the same time it has a certain effectiveness as decoration.

Gould.

What is it that makes these so fundamentally different from nearly all the works—and especially our own—that have followed them? The question may seem naïve. Social and stylistic historians, economists, chemists and psychologists have spent their lives defining and explaining this and many other differences between individual artists, periods, and whole cultures. Such research is invaluable, but its complexity often hides from us two simple, very obvious facts. The first is that it is our own culture, not foreign ones, which can teach us the keenest lessons: the culture of individualist humanism which began in Italy in the thirteenth century. And the second fact is that, at least in painting, a fundamental break occurred in this culture two and a half centuries after it began. After the sixteenth century artists were more psychologically profound (Rembrandt), more successfully ambitious (Rubens), more evocative (Claude); but they also lost an ease and a visual directness which precluded all pretentions; they lost what Berenson called 'tactile values'. After 1600 the great artists, pushed by lonely compulsion, stretch and extend the range of painting, break down its frontiers. Watteau breaks out towards music, Goya towards the stage, Picasso towards pantomime. A few such as Chardin, Corot, Cézanne, did accept the strictest limitations. But before 1550 every artist did. One of the most important results of this difference is that in the great later forays only genius could triumph: before even a small talent could give profound pleasure.

Berger.

No. 89: Carpaccio: *Crucifixion on Mt. Ararat.*

Room III
No. 102: Basaiti: *Saint George and Dragon.*

Room IV
No. 588: Mantegna: *Saint George.*

No. 47: Piero della Francesca: *Saint Jerome.*
No. 628: Cosimo Tura: *Madonna and Child.*
No. 613: Giovanni Bellini: *Madonna, Saint Catherine and the Magdalen.*
No. 586: Memling: *Portrait of a Youth.*
No. 610: Giovanni Bellini: *Madonna, Saint Paul and Saint George.*
No. 881: Giovanni Bellini: *Madonna and Child.*
No. 883: Giovanni Bellini: *Pietà.*
No. 612: Giovanni Bellini: *Madonna.*
No. 596: Giovanni Bellini: *Madonna of the Little Trees.*
No. 594: Giovanni Bellini: *Child Blessing.*
No. 595: Giovanni Bellini: *Allegorical Panels.*

Bellini's five small allegorical panels were painted about 1490 for the frame of an elaborate mirror.

> In the most recent study of his work, Edgar Wind interprets them as a contrast between virtuous love (*Fortuna Amoris*) and its reward (*Cornes Virtutis*) on the one hand and, on the other, anguish (*Servitudo Acediae*) and vain illusions (*Vana Gloria*), the consequence of sinful love, represented by a woman holding a mirror. The four figures are accompanied by a blind harpy representing *Nemesis* (Revenge). These learned allusions which recur in the 16th century books of emblems, which were perhaps chosen to suggest the good and bad uses that can be made of a mirror.
>
> *Chastel.*

No. 915: Giorgione: *The Tempest.*

> The Venetian had as a rule very little personal religion, and consequently did not care for pictures that moved him to contrition or devotion. He preferred to have some pleasantly coloured thing that would put him into a mood connected with the side of life he most enjoyed—with refined merrymaking, with country parties, or with the sweet dreams of youth. Venetian painting alone among Italian schools was ready to satisfy such a demand, and it thus became the first genuinely modern art: for the most vital difference that can be indicated between the arts in antiquity and modern times is this; that now the arts tend to address themselves more and more to the actual needs of men, while in olden times they were supposed to serve some more than human purpose.
>
> The pictures required for a house were naturally of a different kind for those suited to the Council Hall or the School, where large paintings, which could be filled with many figures, were in place. For the house smaller pictures were necessary, such as

could easily be carried about. The mere dimensions, therefore, excluded pageants but, in any case, the pageant was too formal a subject to suit all moods—too much like a brass band always playing in the room. The easel picture had to be without too definite a subject, and could no more permit being translated into words than a sonata.

Giorgione combined the fine feeling and poetry of Bellini with Carpaccio's gaiety and love of beauty and colour. Stirred with the enthusiasms of his own generation as people who have lived through other phases of feeling could not be, Giorgione painted pictures so perfectly in touch with the ripened spirit of the Renaissance that they met with the success which those things only find that at the same moment wake us to the full sense of a need and satisfy it.

Giorgione's life was short and very few of his works—not a score in all—have escaped destruction. But these suffice to give us a glimpse into that brief moment when the Renaissance found its most genuine expression in painting.

Our real interest in Italian painting is at bottom an interest in that art which we almost instinctively feel to have been the fittest expression found by a period in that history of modern Europe which has much in common with youth. The Renaissance has the fascination of those years when we seemed so full of promise both with ourselves and to everybody else.

Berenson.

The small picture known as the *Tempest*—which is one of only two or three whose attribution to Giorgione has never been doubted and which on the strength of an inscription on the back of a comparable painting now at Vienna probably dates from around 1506—is the quintessence of the Giorgionesque. For centuries its subject defeated all who tried to read a meaning into it, but X-rays have recently shown that there was originally a further female form in the place now occupied by the young man and for this reason (since two such different characters could hardly be interchangeable) it seems most logical to assume that no specific 'story' is being told and that the whole is a fantasy. Such, indeed, is its mood. Nothing like it has been painted before, and its strangeness and unearthly beauty is still potent after four centuries. The naked woman suckling her child, half watched by the (fully dressed) young man standing impassively as if on guard, a pair of broken columns (with an extra brick at the base of their plinth merely for pictorial reasons), part of an improbable building on the left, the bridge over the torrent (which may or may not be continuous with the water in the foreground: we have no means of deciding), more buildings (including one with an oriental dome) in the background, and a stormy sky overhead—the whole thing has the fantastic inconsequence of a dream, and this may, indeed, provide some clue to its origin. For not long before, in 1499, a curious romance, the *Hypnerotomachia Poliphili*, had been published at Venice and widely read. In this the conduct of all human affairs is likened to a dream, and a dream-like quality informs much of its narrative. One of its plates shows ruined columns as in the Tempest, and although the painting can hardly be regarded as an actual illustration of the book it may well be that Giorgione had had the Hypnerotomachia in mind shortly before painting this extraordinary and beautiful work.

Gould.

One day the episode here illustrated may be identified—the story, perhaps, of a mother of some future hero, who was cast out of the city into the wilderness with her child and was there discovered by a friendly young shepherd. For this, it seems, is what Giorgione wanted to represent. But it is not due to its content that the picture is one of the most wonderful things in art. Though the figures are not particularly carefully drawn, and though the composition is somewhat artless, the picture is clearly blended into a whole simply by the light and air that permeates it all. It is the weird light of a thunderstorm and for the first time, it seems, the landscape before which the actors of the picture move is not just a background. It is there, by its own right, as the real subject of the painting. We look from the figures to the scenery which fills the major part of the small panel, and then back again, and we feel somehow that unlike his predecessors and contemporaries, Giorgione has not drawn things and persons to arrange them afterwards in space, but that he really thought of nature, the earth, the trees, the light, air and clouds and the human beings with their cities and bridges as one. In a way, this was almost as big a step forward into a new realm as the inventions of perspective had been. From now on, painting was more than drawing plus colouring. It was an art with its own secret laws and devices.

Gombrich.

No. 272: Giorgione: *Old Woman.*

The Portrait of an Old Woman in the Academy, generally attributed to him, displays a startling realism and an attention to detail rather far removed from Giorgione's usual manner and reminiscent of Northern painting.

Chastel.

89

I feel tempted to let my fancy run free, and to weave the plot of a romance around these two pictures, the *Soldier and Gypsy* or *Tempesta* and the *Old Woman 'Col Tempo'*. The soldier would be the young Giorgione himself looking on while the somewhat more mature woman was giving suck to his and her child. She may be suffering a revulsion of feeling against him for having brought her to this pass, and he painted her as she would look when old, as an admonition to gather roses while she might for time was aflying.

Berenson.

Room VI
No. 291: Bonifacio: *Dives and Lazurus*.

The elegant figures in the vestibule of a beautiful C16 Venetian villa are contrasted with the figure of the beggar in the foreground, and seem unaware of the conflagration in the background: the subject matter does little more than offer the occasion for this painter's virtuoso handling of colour and light.

Room VII
No. 912: Lorenzo Lotto: *Portrait of a Young Man in his Study*.

Toward the middle of the sixteenth century, when elsewhere in Italy painting was trying to adapt itself to the hypocrisy of a Church whose chief reason for surviving as an institution was that it helped Spain to subject the world to tyranny, and when portraits were already exhibiting the fascinating youths of an earlier generation turned into obsequious and elegant courtiers—in Venice painting kept true to the ripened and more reflective spirit which succeeded to the most glowing decades of the Renaissance. This led men to take themselves more seriously, to act with more consideration of consequences, and to think of life with less hope and exultation. Quieter joys were sought, the pleasures of friendship and of the affections. Life not having proved the endless holiday it had promised to be, earnest people began to question whether under the gross masque of the official religion there was not something to console them for departed youth and for the failure of hopes. Thus religion began to revive in Italy, this time not ethnic nor political, but personal—an answer to the real needs of the human soul.

It is scarcely to be wondered at that the Venetian artist in whom we first find the expression of the new feelings, should have been one who by wide travel had been brought in contact with the miseries of Italy in a way not possible for those who had remained sheltered in Venice. Lorenzo Lotto, when he is most himself, does

90

not paint the triumph of man over his environment, but in his altar pieces, and even more in his portraits, he shows us people in want of the consolation of religion, of sober thought, of friendship and affection. They look out from his canvasses as if begging for sympathy.

Berenson.

Titian and Tintoretto represent their sitters erect, stately and at their best or better than their best, as what they wanted to be taken for rather than as what, in their hearts, they knew themselves to be. In other words, Titian and Tintoretto painted ceremonial portraits and, but for the grace of genius, anticipated the effigies still perpetrated annually in the Royal Academy of London. Not so *Lotto*. Already in his earliest portraits *Lotto* could portray individuals, not mere types: individuals with personal preoccupations and feelings, and with moods of their own. Through a career of 60 years he was always painting what was most peculiarly characteristic in the sitter at the moment he was portraying him. Psychological snapshots? Yes, if you like, but serious, grave even, and stylized by art and never common, let alone vulgar, as in the performances of some of his Northern contemporaries. Scarcely any other artist can offer the variety of types that we discover in the portraits of *Lorenzo Lotto*. It almost would seem as if he had acquired the reputation of being the artist able to portray the kind of individual, who for personal, social or financial reasons, did not want to employ, or could not afford to employ—a Titian or Tintoretto.

On the other hand his sensitiveness gave him an appreciation of shades of feeling that would have escaped Titian's notice. Titian never painted a single figure that does not have the look and bearing, rank and circumstance require. His people are well-bred, dignified, conforming perfectly to current standards. We cannot find fault with Titian for having painted nothing but prosperity, beauty and health—men on parade, as it were—but the interest he himself arouses in the world he painted, makes us eager to know more of these people than he tells us: to know them more intimately, in their own house, if possible, subject to the wear and tear of ordinary existence. We long to know how they take life, what they think and, above all, what they feel; Titian tells us none of these things, and if we are to satisfy our curiosity, we must turn to Lotto, who is as personal as Titian is typical. If artists were at all conscious of their aims in the 16th century as they are supposed to be now, we might imagine Titian asking of every person he was going to paint: '*Who are you? What is your position in society?*' while *Lotto* would put the question: '*What sort of person are you? How do you take life?*'

Berenson.

91

Returning to Room VI
   On easel by exit doorway No. 314: Titian: *John the Baptist*.

Room X
   No. 725: Tintoretto: *Jesus Presented at the Temple*.
   No. 400: Titian: *Pietà*.
   No. 213: Tintoretto: *Crucifixion*.
   No. 245: Tintoretto: *Portrait of Soranzo*.

Titian was too busy with commissions for foreign princes to supply the great demand there was (for portraits) in Venice alone. Not only with much of the air of good breeding of Titian's likenesses, but with even greater splendour, and with an astonishing rapidity of execution. The Venetian portrait, it will be remembered was expected to be more than a likeness. It was expected to give pleasure to the eye, and to stimulate emotions. Tintoretto was ready to give ample satisfaction to all such expectations. His portraits, although they are not so individualised as Lotto's, nor such close studies of character as Titian's, always render the man at his best, in glowing health, full of life and determination. They give us the sensuous pleasure we get from jewels, and at the same time they make us look back with amazement to a State where the human plant was in such vigour as to produce old men of the kind represented in most of Tintoretto's portraits.

Berenson.

No. 31: Tintoretto: *Carrying off Body of Saint Mark*.
No. 42: Tintoretto: *Saint Mark Rescues Slave from Torture*.

Tintoretto's great picture of the 'Miracle of Saint Mark' was painted between 1544 and 1548, before he was thirty. The story tells that a pious slave, forbidden by his master to visit and venerate the house of Saint Mark, disobeyed the command and went. As a punishment his master ordered him to be blinded and maimed; but the hands of the executioner were miraculously stayed and their weapons refused to act. The master, looking on, was naturally at once converted. . . .

An interesting derivative detail of the work is the gateway at the back over which the sculptured figures recline, for these obviously were suggested by casts, which we know Tintoretto to have possessed, of Michael Angelo's tombs in S. Lorenzo's sacristy at Florence. Every individual in the picture is alive and breathing, but none more remarkably so than the woman on the left with a child in her arms and her knee momentarily resting on a slope of the pillar. No doubt some of the crowd are drawn, after the fashion

92

of the time, from public men in Venice; but I know not if they can now be identified.

Lucas.

No. 203: Veronese: *Feast of the House of Levy.*

Verona, being a dependency of Venice, did no ruling and certainly not at all so much thinking as Venice, and life there continued healthful, simple, unconscious, untroubled by the approaching storm of the world's feelings. But although thought and feeling may be slow in invading a town, fashion comes there quickly. Spanish fashions in dress, and Spanish ceremonial in manner reached Verona soon enough, and in Paolo Caliari [Veronese] we find all these fashions reflected, but health, simplicity, and unconsciousness as well. This combination of seemingly opposite qualities forms his great charm for us to-day, and it must have proved as great an attraction to many of the Venetians of his own time, for they were already far enough removed from simplicity to appreciate to the full his singularly happy combination of ceremony and splendour with an almost childlike naturalness of feeling . . . it is curious to note that Paolo's chief employers were the monasteries. His cheerfulness, and his frank and joyous worldliness, the qualities, in short, which we find in his huge pictures of feasts, seem to have been particularly welcome to those who were expected to make their meat and drink of the very opposite qualities. This is no small comment on the times, and shows how thorough had been the permeation of the spirit of the Renaissance, when even the religious orders gave up their pretence to asceticism and piety.

Berenson.

The measure of the anachronism of Veronese's art is clearly indicated by the fact that one of his pictures, the vast *'Feast in the House of Simon'*, was the occasion of his being arraigned before the Inquisition. For it seems in the first place anachronistic that anyone so urbane and perfectly balanced as Veronese (to judge by his work) should even be contemporary with such an institution. Furthermore, it is quite clear from the trial to what extent his picture, which we may perhaps regard as his masterpiece, was out of keeping with the official ecclesiastical requirements of the time. The minutes of the trial, by remarkable good fortune, are preserved and constitute fascinating first-hand evidence of the painter's intentions.

The gist of the Inquisitors' complaint was that in this picture Veronese had painted a dog, when the Scriptures said there should be a Magdalen, and that he had introduced figures of German soldiers, buffoons and dwarfs for which there was no warrant in the biblical source at all. Veronese begins his defence by saying that since Simon, the owner of the house, was a rich man it is likely that he would have had numerous servants. But when questioned specifically about the buffoon with the parrot (left centre) he says categorically that he merely put it in for the purposes of decoration, that the canvas was a large one and that he considered himself at liberty to introduce such additional figures as he pleased.

The fact that in the end Veronese was ordered to make changes in the picture (which he did merely by changing the title to 'Feast in the House of Levi') is the least significant part of the affair. What is more interesting is the painter's attitude as revealed in his evidence. It is virtually that of the Renaissance. It takes beauty as its criterion rather than that spiritual forcefulness which was 'de rigueur' in this, the strictest period of the Counter-Reformation. (1573) And, indeed, the picture has every quality of High Renaissance art. The composition in its parallel planes, is as rational as that of the School of Athens and the individual figures so easy and graceful in their movements. The lighting is clear, pale and lucid, in contrast to Tintoretto's magical illumination and (sometimes) his bright orange skies. The whole accent is on worldly splendour —on the magnificence of the aristocratic life with fine furnishings and superb velvet and silk clothes and set against a palatial background. The architecture portrayed, indeed, has an interest of its own in view of Veronese's historical position. The main arcade, with its ample half-columns and its sculptured spandrels, is in an idiom which started with Sansovino's library at Venice and was developed by Sanmicheli and by Palladio.

Gould.

No. 217: Tintoretto: *Deposition.*

In some ways the clearest impression of the essential strangeness of Tintoretto's art, both in its formal characteristics and in its content, may be derived from a comparison of his version of the '*Intombment of Christ*' with that by Titian.* Both pictures may be considered masterpieces but they display the most extreme differences of approach.

Titian disposes his figures fairly closely but there is not the slightest uncertainty of the relative positions of any of them. The feet of the three male bearers are clearly seen and we can also see exactly how the Mary's on the left relate to them. But in Tintoretto's picture the figures are densely compressed. . . . We cannot see how there would be space for them all, nor are we meant to do so. Furthermore Tintoretto uses a disquieting device to bring us

* No. 400, beyond entrance door.

94

in close contact with the subject. . . . The drapery under Christ's feet comes almost to the edge of the picture, so that His feet themselves would actually project through the picture plane. The contrast in the content of the two pictures is even more striking. Titian shows us a variety of emotions—the bearer holding Christ's feet displays a stoical grief, St. John behind is almost overcome and turns away. The Virgin advances timidly and pathetically, her trembling mouth slightly open. The Magdalen faces the body with a troubled but firmer expression. With Tintoretto there is not only no contrast of expression, no emotion is shown on the faces at all. His figures are abstractions. Several of the faces are strongly fore-shortened or in shadow, and where we can see them clearly they are masks. . . . Even with the hands, which can often be used not only as an adjunct to facial expression but even as a substitute for it, Tintoretto makes but little play. Those of the male Saint are concealed, like his features, those of the Mary who stands at the foot of the Cross make a completely impersonal gesture of despair, while the Madonna's right, though very impressive in its context, is as limp and expressionless as her face. The emotional impact, which is very great, of the picture as a whole derives from this very passivity, from the grouping of the figures in space and from the dramatic and mysterious illumination, and this in general is the rule with Tintoretto.

The denial implicit in this attitude of the importance of man as an individual together with the utter other-worldliness of the world created by Tintoretto's fantastic light, isolates his art alike from that of the Renaissance and the Baroque. To the Renaissnace, man is a noble creature and each representative of the race a unique creation. To the Baroque, man is a hero, bigger, stronger and more vigorous than life and not subject to petty failings. In both cases the world he inhabits is healthy, sunlit and lacking in mysterious or ghostly implications. In both cases, too, human emotions, such as bravery, fear, pride, or humility, even if stereotyped in accordance with the idiom of the Grand Manner, are an essential part of the respective languages. But to Tintoretto, man is of no consequence as an individual. His personal emotions are minimized because they are of the smallest importance. He is merely one of a nameless herd of puppets who carry out the destiny imposed on them by God.

Gould.

No. 1324: Veronese: *Marriage of Saint Catherine.*
No. 260: Veronese: *Annunciation.*
No. 751: Luca Giordano: *Crucifixion.*
No. 837: G. B. Tiepolo: *Spandrel with Architecture and Praying Figures.*
No. 462: G. B. Tiepolo: *Saint Helena Discovering Cross.*

No. 836: G. B. Tiepolo: *Spandrel.*
No. 643: Luca Giordano: *Deposition.*
No. 41: Tintoretto: *Cain and Abel.*
No. 252: Bassano: *Raising of Lazarus.*

At an early date the Venetians had perfected an art in which there is scarcely any intellectual content whatever, and in which colour, jewel-like or opaline, is almost everything. Venetian glass was at the same time an outcome of the Venetians' love of sensuous beauty and a continual stimulant to it. Pope Paul II, for example, who was a Venetian, took such a delight in the colour and glow of jewels, that he was always looking at them and always handling them. When painting, accordingly, had reached the point where it was no longer dependent upon the Church, nor even expected to be decorative, but when it was used purely for pleasure, the day could not be far distant when people would expect painting to give them the same enjoyment they received from jewels and glass. In Bassano's works this taste found full satisfaction. Most of his pictures seem at first as dazzling, then as cooling and soothing, as the best kind of stained glass; while the colouring of details, particularly of those under high lights, is jewel-like, as clear and deep and satisfying as rubies and emeralds.

It need scarcely be added after all that has been said about light and atmosphere in connection with Titian and Tintoretto, and their handling of real life, that Bassano's treatment of both was even more masterly. If this were not so, neither picture-fanciers of his own time, nor we nowadays, should care for his works as we do. They represent life in far more humble phases than even the pictures of Tintoretto, and, without recompensing effects of light and atmosphere, they would not be more enjoyable than the cheap work of the smaller Dutch master. It must be added, too, that without his jewel-like colouring, Bassano would often be no more delightful than Teniers.

Berenson.

Room XIII (on right of corridor)
  No. 234: Tintoretto: *Portrait of a Procuratore.*
  No. 233: Tintoretto: *Portrait of Doge Alvise Mocenigo.*
  No. 897: Tintoretto: *Portrait of a Procuratore.*

Room XVII (on left of corridor)
  No. 497: Bellotto: *School of San Marco.*
  No. 463: Canaletto: *Portico.*

Here the motifs are not specifically Venetian at all and Canaletto turns back to the theatrical architectural settings of his youth, though sprinkling the scene still with touches of genre—like the woman sitting sewing on the right. There is no obvious effort at fantasy or picturesqueness; the intention is rather to invent an impressive vista in the grand manner, splendidly lit, and based on the dignified principles of perspective.

. . . Algarotti had employed Canaletto on those unions of invention and fact which put the Rialto, the Pantheon and some ruins all together in a caprice setting. Canaletto's '*morceau de reception*' is something much more ambitious, though not unique in his late work: the creation of a scene which shall appear realistic but which is in fact totally invented. The result, large, elaborate, carefully designed and carefully painted, now seem to us (not surprisingly) academic.

Levey.

No. 709: Guardi: *View of San Giorgio.*

Guardi has completely mastered the effects that had been studied by seventeenth century painters. He has learned that, once we are given the general impression of a scene, we are quite ready to supply and supplement the details ourselves. If we look closely at his gondoliers we discover, to our surprise, that they are made up simply of a few deftly placed coloured patches yet if we step back the illusion becomes completely effective.

Gombrich.

No. 741: Pittoni: *Romans Sacking Temple at Jerusalem.*

Pittoni was probably considered rather 'learned' and he presents an architectural setting more elaborate than most contemporary painters would have been capable of thinking up. Certainly in eighteenth century France elaborate classical subjects often had to be planned between the painter and the Academie des Belles-Lettres. Architectural settings, especially classical ones, were well worth the trouble of delineating, and Madam Geoffrin speaks for her age when she says of a picture Vien had been commissioned to paint, 'Temples always make a fine effect by enriching pictures'. The architecture in Pittoni's painting lends it additional value. The subject also is very noticeably drawn from history rather than mythology; it is a good deal more serious and elevated than the love-and-duty themes which were no doubt more popular with Venetian taste. But it remains a moment of high drama, and offers striking contrast between the looting Roman soldiery and the distraught aged priests: it is still an emotional depiction, a clash of will, and the despoiling of an ancient civilization by a more modern one.

Levey.

No. 743: Amigoni: *Venus and Adonis.*

The *Venus and Adonis* probably dates from his last stay in Venice, between 1740–47, by which time he was no longer a pioneer of anything, and a fresh generation of younger men had formulated a more truly rococo style. Against the new manner, almost exaggerated in its airy elegancies and light-filled compositions, Amigoni's canvases seem naïve and rather Flemish, and sadly unpoetical. And though Walpole is often unfair and obtuse in his comments on foreign painters, when he speaks of Amigoni's manner as a 'still fainter imitation of that nerveless master Sebastian Ricci' and complains that his figures are 'entirely without expression', it is impossible not to feel that he has put one's objections very well.

Levey.

Nos. 761–9: Longhi: *Pictures of Venetian Life.*
No. 466: Longhi: *A Concert.*

The paint surface is messy, as so often in Longhi; time and practice never taught him how to apply paint. . . .

There is a sort of candour in the slightly ridiculous trio of musical amateurs and a sort of pungency in the pair of clerical card-players, one thin and eager, the other fat and porcinely benevolent. . . .

Because he is unique it has been presumed that he is invaluable. But it seems as if his clumsy handling of paint, his inability ever to establish the planes of a picture, and his incapacity to draw properly, were honest defects that he could not overcome even after many years of practice.

His pictures are therefore, with all their undoubted charm, lazy little pictures: just as the society he pictures is lazy. The world he sees is in general the enclosed one of affluent people trying to pass the time. The rooms they inhabit are enclosed too, and always windowless; they themselves are barely in contact with each other but are placed, like dolls, in a proximity physical rather than emotional.

Levey.

Opposite are some portraits by **Rosalba Carriera.**

Corridor XIX
No. 107: Basaiti (attr.): *Saint Jerome.*

No. 645: Basaiti (attr.): *Portrait*.

No. 90: Carpaccio: *Meeting*.

No. 91: Carpaccio: *Vision of the Crucifixion*.

No. 68: Basaiti: *Apostle James*.

No. 600: Boccaccio Boccacini: *Marriage of Saint Catherine*.

Room XX

No. 567: Gentile Bellini: *Procession of the Cross in the Piazza*.

The great picture by Gentile Bellini, which shows the progress of the Holy Cross procession across the Piazza in 1496, is historically of much interest. One sees many changes and much that is still familiar. The only mosaic on the façade of St. Mark's which still remains is that in the arch over the left door; and that also is the only arch which has been left concave. The three flagstaffs are there, but they have wooden pediments and no lions on the top, as now. The Merceria clock tower is not yet, and the south arcade comes flush with the campanile's north wall; but I doubt if that was so.* The miracle of that year was the healing of a youth who had been fatally injured in the head; his father may be seen kneeling just behind the relic.

Lucas.

No. 568: Gentile Bellini: *The Miracle of the Cross*.

The Miracle of the Cross . . . depicts the leader of the Brotherhood, Andrea Vendramin, later to become Doge, in the act of miraculously recovering the relics of the Holy Cross that had fallen into the San Lorenzo during a procession.

Gentile Bellini describes the incident with a charmingly observant story-teller's talent. The figures in the foreground remind us that he is also a shrewd portraitist.

Chastel.

For Gentile Bellini, whose keen eye recorded exactly what he saw, Venice was still a purely Gothic city; witness his famous picture (1500) of the True Cross being retrieved from the Canale di San Lorenzo by Andrea Vendramin (Gallerie dell'Accademia, Venice). This was too prosaic for Carpaccio who, when painting the same episode only a few years earlier,† though consenting to show the old wooden Rialto Bridge as it really was, fantastically

* This licence enables us to see the *Porta della Carta* and part of the Ducal Palace though they are of course in fact hidden from view at this point.

† No. 566.

99

surmounted by funnel-shaped Gothic chimneys and roof gardens, could not resist the impulse to embellish the foreground by adding a loggia of his own invention—an open gallery typical of the new architecture practised by Coducci.

Pignatti.

... the Renaissance was a period in the history of modern Europe comparable to youth in the life of the individual. It had all youth's love of finery and of play. The more people were imbued with the new spirit, the more they loved pageants. The pageant was an outlet for many of the dominant passions of the time for there a man could display all the finery he pleased, satisfy his love of antiquity by masquerading as Caesar or Hannibal, his love of knowledge by finding out how the Romans dressed and rode in triumph, his love of glory by the display of wealth and skill in the management of the ceremony, and, above all, his love of feeling himself alive. Solemn writers have not disdained to describe to the minutest details many of the pageants which they witnessed.

Venice, too, knew the love of glory, and the passion was perhaps only the more intense because it was all dedicated to the State. There was nothing the Venetians would not do to add to its greatness, glory, and splendour. It was this which led them to make of the city itself that wondrous monument to the love and awe they felt for their Republic, which still rouses more admiration and gives more pleasure than any other one achievement of the art-impulse in man. They were not content to make their city the most beautiful in the world; they performed ceremonies in its honour partaking of all the solemnity of religious rites. Processions and pageants by land and by sea, free from that gross element of improvisation which characterised them elsewhere in Italy, formed no less a part of the functions of the Venetian State than the High Mass in the Catholic Church. Such a function with Doge and Senators arrayed in gorgeous costumes no less prescribed than the raiments of ecclesiastics, in the midst of the fairy-like architecture of the Piazza or canals, was the event most eagerly looked forward to, and the one that gave most satisfaction to the Venetian's love of his State, and to his love of splendour, beauty, and gaiety. He would have had them every day if it were possible, and to make up for their rarity, he loved to have representations of them. So most Venetian pictures at the beginning of the sixteenth century tended to take the form of magnificent processions, if they did not actually represent them. They are processions in the Piazza, as in Gentile Bellini's 'Corpus Christi' picture, or on the water, as in Carpaccio's picture where St. Ursula leaves her home; or they represent what was a gorgeous but common sight in

Venice, the reception or dismissal of ambassadors, as in several pictures of Carpaccio's St. Ursula series.*. . .

The Mutual Aid Societies—the Schools, as they were called—were not long in getting the masters who were employed in the Doge's Palace to execute for their own meeting places pictures equally splendid.

Many of these pictures—most in fact—took the form of pageants; but even in such, intended as they were for almost domestic purposes, the style of high ceremonial was relaxed, and elements taken directly from life were introduced. In his 'Corpus Christi'† Gentile Bellini paints not only the solemn and dazzling procession in the Piazza, but the elegant young men who strut about in all their finery, the foreign loungers and even the unfailing beggar by St. Mark's. In 'The Miracle of the True Cross' he introduces gondoliers taking care to bring out all the beauty of their lithe, comely figures as they stand to ply the oar, and does not reject even such an episode as a serving-maid standing in a doorway watching a negro who is about to plunge into the canal. He treats this bit of the picture with all the charm and much of that delicate feeling for simple effects of light and colour that we find in such Dutch painters as Vermeer van Delft and Peter de Hoogh.

Berenson.

The genius of Giovanni Bellini seems to us now so outstanding, and his influence in the Veneto during the opening years of the 16th century so pre-eminent, that it is at first difficult to realise that during the greater part of his life his fame had been eclipsed by that of his brother, Gentile. The latter would have appeared unquestionably the most eminent Venetian painter working in the second half of the century. He was knighted by the Emperor in 1469, summoned by the Sultan to Constantinople ten years later and entrusted with the most important commission in the power of the Venetian State to give—the decoration of the great hall in the Doge's palace. These paintings were destroyed by fire in the 16th century, but sufficient of Gentile's work in general survives to permit us to estimate his talents.

The role played by religion in the Venetian state at the time of the Renaissance was of a uniquely possessive character. . . . This tendency to identify his State with the Christian religion represented one side of the Venetian's character. Another, its love of luxury and general sensuality, is shown in the opulent splendour of the city itself, with its accent on rich materials—many coloured marbles and gold mosaic externally, and gilded wood, damasks

* Room 21.   † No. 567.

and fantastic metal-work and glass in its interiors—and above all, in the pageants which then, as now, served as an occasion for the whole city to flock to the route. As these were usually religious in character they thus combined the two most characteristic elements in Venetian life and we may therefore not be surprised at the popularity of portrayals of them in art. Those of Gentile Bellini were the prototypes, and though we can see from them that he had no fraction of his brother's greatness, his minutely careful rendering of the splendour of Venetian ceremonial was precisely what the circumstances of the moment demanded.

Gould.

No. 566: Carpaccio: *The Miracle of the Cross at the Rialto.*

The painting is a valuable reconstruction of the Grand Canal as it was at the end of the 15th century.

The miracle (the healing of a possessed soul) takes place in a loggia decorated with the Roman medallions that were then the last word in 'Classical style' as conceived by the Lombard sculptors; the Vendramin-Calergi Palace which still has its portal decorated with profiles of Roman emperors, is a fine example of this fashion. This type of decorative motif recurs frequently in Carpaccio's works.

The *Miracle at the Rialto* shows the old drawbridge still in existence at the time, the curious silhouettes of the chimneys and the squat gondolas whose shape was to be modified in the 17th century.

Chastel.

These three pictures [in this room] are valuable for the light they throw on the way in which Venetians dressed during the Renaissance and their behaviour in official ceremonies. They show us the 'fair-haired men with slim figures, grave, silent tread and careful speech' described by Burckhardt. In this they differed from the other peoples of Italy; to some extent Nordic in their ways, they were nevertheless apt to dress with all the ostentation of orientals when they were not wearing their uniforms of office—which remained unchanged from the Middle Ages to the 18th century.

The normal dress of the solemn, middle-aged patricians of Venice bore no resemblance to the garish and luxurious costume which so delighted the young men of the time. Basically they dressed in a long gown of black cloth, revealing the collar of a white shirt above the neck clasp. This heavy garment with its wide folds was also worn by the men of the professional classes, and as it reached right to the ground, those who wore it were obliged to walk with a slow, solemn, dignified step. This was the characteristic walk of the bourgeoisie and the aristocracy at a time when only children and workmen were so indiscreet as to run in the streets. On ceremonial occasions, Senators wore gowns of crimson satin, for this was the distinguishing mark of their office.

Brion.

Room XXI (left along corridor)
Carpaccio: *Dream of Saint Ursula.*

All the architecture of the series is delightful, as well as being realistically conceived in terms of space and structure. Most of the buildings are of course invented, but some are based on real ones: the Ducal Palace appears in No. 573; in No. 575, the palace on the right plainly owes something to the Cá d'Oro (p. 149), and the towers are based on those of Rhodes and Candia, known from late C15 engravings.

No. 572: Arrival of the English Ambassadors to propose the marriage between the King's son and Princess Ursula. In her bedroom, Ursula tells her father she intends to go on a pilgrimage.

No. 573: The King of Bretagna gives his reply to the Ambassadors.

No. 574: The Ambassadors take the reply to England. As Hare remarks, the Venetian idea of England is interesting.

No. 575: The Departure.

> Here are three representations. On the right is Ursula with her father, on the left Conon with his. In the centre the pair meet near the ship of their pilgrimage. The background is supposed to give the characteristics of a civilised and a barbaric city.
>
> *Hare.*

No. 577: The Engaged Couple arrive in Rome—the Castle of S. Angel in the background.

No. 578: The Dream of Saint Ursula. As a girl, she had dreamed that she would devote herself to the service of God.

No. 579: The arrival at Cologne, which is being beseiged by the Huns.

No. 580: The Martyrdom of the Christians, and the Funeral of Ursula.

No. 576: Apotheosis of Ursula.

> Certain of the episodes from the cycle painted for the Scuola di Sant'Orsola contain charming descriptions of Venetian interiors of Carpaccio's time.
>
> In the scene showing Ursula and her father* there is a canopied

---

* No. 572, right.

bed with embroidered drapery near the picture of the Virgin and Child in a precious frame. And the room where Saint Ursula lies sleeping* with the flowers on the sill beneath the small, lead-set window-panes, an open book on the table and a candle stick hung in front of some devotional painting, is the room of a well-bred girl who says her prayers and sets her slippers near her bed before going to sleep. Beyond the doorway, another lighted aperture creates a skilful light effect in the Flemish manner.

The story of St. Ursula is theoretically an illustration of the fabulous career of the saint, but it has always been recognised as providing as accurate a picture of contemporary Venetian life as the avowed representations of ceremonials. One sees how much Carpaccio learnt from Gentile, yet the pedestrian quality of the latter's arrangement of figures in rows is transformed by Giovanni's light which brings to life the different textures of rich brocades, carpets and pearls, of water shimmering in the sun or cool and transparent in the shadows.

At the same time the increase in pictorial quality is accompanied by a decrease in solemnity. Gentile's figures have always a due sense of the occasion, are always to some extent absorbed in the religious ceremony, no matter how far away from it they may be. But Carpaccio's ladies and gentlemen lounge amorously in gondolas, or indulge in trivial conversation or gossip during a solemn moment. If documentation has become suffused with an element of poetry it would also be true to say that history has become genre.

Gould.

Much as he loved pageants, he loved homelier scenes as well. His 'Dream of St. Ursula'† shows us a young girl asleep in a room filled with the quiet morning light. Indeed, it may be better described as the picture of a room with the light playing softly upon its walls, upon the flower-pots in the window, and upon the writing-table and the cupboards. A young girl happens to be asleep in the bed, but the picture is far from being a merely economic illustration of this episode in the life of the saint. Again, let us take the work in the same series‡ where King Maure dismisses the ambassadors. Carpaccio has made this a scene of a chancellery in which the most striking features are neither the king, nor the ambassadors, but the effect of the light that streams through a side door on the left and a poor clerk labouring at his task.

Carpaccio's quality is the quality of the painter of 'genre' of which he was the earliest Italian master. His 'genre' differs from

* No. 578.   † No. 578.   ‡ No. 573.

104

Dutch or French not in kind but in degree. Dutch 'genre' is much more democratic, and, as painting, is of a far finer quality, but it deals with its subject, as Carpaccio does, for the sake of its own pictorial capacities and for the sake of the effects of colour and of light and shade.

Berenson.

Room XXII (return along corridor)
No. 592: Cima da Conegliano: *Tobias and Angel.*
No. 604: Cima da Conegliano: *Deposition.*
No. 603: Cima da Conegliano: *Madonna and Child.*

Behind first screen
Nos. 83, 84, 86: Benedetto Diana: *Madonna and Saints.*

On second screen
No. 82: Benedetto Diana: *Madonna and Saints*

On right wall beside second screen
No. 823: Lazzaro Bastiani: *Funeral of Saint Jerome.*

Behind second screen
No. 618: Alvise Vivarini: *John the Baptist.*
No. 607: Alvise Vivarini: *Sacred Conversation.*

Alvise was a rather crude, but forceful painter. There is no finesse in his draughtsmanship, and his colours are muddy. But he seems to have had a passion for the 3-dimensional element, and used the discoveries in lighting to this end. His Child is so plastic that combined with the unrefined draughtsmanship, He looks like a rubber figure blown up to bursting point. By shutting out the background, furthermore (by means of the curtain) and crowding the strongly-lit figures closely together round the Madonna's throne (itself very narrow) as though, having insufficient space within the picture, they would burst out on to the spectator, one is uncomfortably aware of the 3-dimensional element as if one were looking through stereoscopic spectacles.

Gould.

Nos. 593, 593a, 619: Alvise Vivarini: *Saints.*

On right wall beside second screen
No. 103: Crivelli: *Saints Jerome and Augustine.*
No. 103a: Crivelli: *Saints Peter and Paul.*

Central Apse
   Nos. 621, 621a, 621b, 621c: Giovanni Bellini: *Four Triptychs*.

Left Chapel
   No. 105: Crivelli: *Four Saints*.
   No. 100: Bastiani: *Il Presepe*.
   No. 734: Giovanni Bellini: *Annunciation*.

Last Room
   No. 626: Titian: *Presentation of the Virgin*.

A picture remarkable for its perspective and colour tones, suffused with light from the side.

> *The Presentation of the Virgin* . . . started about 1534 . . . which reverts to an older scheme of iconography such as had already been used, among others, by Cima, is (apart from certain works by Veronese) the last major painting entirely in the High Renaissance classical tradition executed anywhere in Italy. It represents, indeed, a strange reversion by Titian after his proto-Baroque phase initiated by the *Assunta*.* The figures, all arranged parallel with the picture plane, are spaced in a completely rational and lucid manner, and the colouring and lighting are all serenity and calm.
>
> *Gould.*

* In the Frari church, p. 155.

(Cannalletto in Maschera)

Il fait bon voir (Magny) ces Coïons magnifiques,
Leur superbe Arcenal, leurs vaisseaux, leur abbord,
Leur Sainct Marc, leur Palais, leur Realte, leur port,
Leur changes, leurs profits, leur banque et leur trafiques.

Il fait bon voir le bec de leurs chapprons antiques,
Leurs robbes à grand'manche et leurs bonnets sans bord,
Leur parler tout grossier, leur gravité, leur port,
Et leurs sages avis aux affaires publiques.

Il fait bon voir de tout leur Senat balloter,
Il fait bon voir par tout leurs gondolles flotter,
Leurs femmes, leurs festins, leur vivre solitaire:

Mais ce que l'on en doit meilleur estimer,
C'est quand ces vieux coquz vont espouser la mer,
Dont ils sont les maris et le Turc l'adultère.   *Du Bellay*.

3

San Zaccaria – Arsenal – Scuola degli Schiavoni

This walk includes the series of paintings by Carpaccio in S. Giorgio degli Schiavoni. They are outstandingly beautiful; if time is very short, hire a gondola and keep it waiting while you see them. The walk begins along the Riva degli Schiavoni—in front of the Ducal Palace. The last two lines in the poem opposite—addressed by Joachim du Bellay to his friend Olivier de Magny—are

> . . . a humourous reference to the famous 'Sposalizio del Mar'—Wedding of the Sea, an annual ceremony of great pomp in which the Doge cast a ring into the Adriatic and paid homage to the seas as the instrument of Venetian wealth and grandeur—and a sly allusion to the rising naval power of the Ottoman Turks, who by then, whether adulterously or not, had virtually supplanted Venice in the fickle graces of the Mediterranean.
>
> *Pignatti.*

Before you cross the Ponte della Paglia you can see on the side of the bridge a little tabernacle with C16 relief—the Madonna of the Gondoliers. Just before the next bridge, on the left—a C15 palazzo now the Danieli Hotel.

> It is true that Alfred de Musset, when he paid a catastrophic visit to Venice with George Sand, who promptly ran off with a handsome young doctor—it is quite true that de Musset occupied Room 13 at the Hotel Danieli ('Alfred was a sad flirt,' said Swinburne, 'and George was no gentleman'.)
>
> *Morris.*

The building is perhaps more distinguished as the site of the performance of the first opera in Venice—Monteverdi's *Proserpina Rapita*.

Go over the bridge, and then left under the archway after Hotel Savoia e Jolanda into a small campo, dominated by the C15 façade of the church of S. Zaccaria.

It is a very tall church, much too tall for its width by the canons of classical architecture, and its Gothic skeleton is barely disguised by an incrustation of Renaissance motifs. Begun by Antonio Gambello in the 1440s, it was completed in the last two decades of the century by Mauro Coducci who designed three tiers of round-headed windows and shell-capped niches crowned by a curious semicircular pediment. It is easy to see how this façade must have appealed to the Venetians, for while it was up to date in classical detail it yet retained the opulent elaboration of the flamboyant Gothic style. But whereas the façade is the result of a successful compromise, the interior suggests a state of hostility. The proportions of this lofty church and its plan—with a screen round the high altar, an ambulatory and apsidal chapels—are Gothic. But most of the decorations are outspokenly Renaissance. Behind the elegant Gothic screen surrounding the high altar there is open warfare, where octagonal Gothic piers suddenly develop into Corinthian half-columns.

Honour.

Inside the church, the columns, capitals and ceiling deserve special notice.

The nave is a very characteristic example of how the Byzantine manner of spreading cycles of paintings like carpets over the walls continued in Venice even in post-Byzantine art. Also modelled on the Eastern church is the Venetian custom of adorning the supporting structures with ornate and costly materials, either permanently or on festive occasions.

Decker.

On right, entrance to Chapel of St. Athanasius (no admission charge; a contribution to be placed in the box).

On Easel
Tintoretto: *Birth of Saint John.*

Over entrance
Van Dyck (attr.): *Crucifixion.*

From this chapel go through to Chapel of St. Tarasius.

Altar piece (from left to right)
G. and A. da Murano: *Saint Mark.*
Plebanus di S. Agnese: *Saint Blaise.*
.Plebanus di S. Agnese: *Virgin.*

Plebanus di S. Agnese: *Saint Martin.*
G. and A. da Murano: *Saint Elisabeth.*

Behind altar (bottom row)
C14 episodes in the life of a saint.

On wall on left of altar
G. and A. da Murano: *Altarpiece.*

The mosaics before the main altar remain from the C12 church; by lifting the trap door at the other end of the chapel, you can see the remains of an older floor (C9). The stairs lead to the Crypt (switch on the wall), the floor may sometimes be under water.

Back into main church, follow the ambulatory round behind the high altar. The apse is decorated with Andrea del Castagno: *Frescoes* representing God the Father, Four Evangelists, St. Zacharias and John the Baptist. The Figures stand out firmly, in the hard-edge, high relief style characteristic of the mid-C15 Florentine style in which del Castagno painted.

> It is extremely interesting for the architecture as Byzantine reminiscences of the past go hand in hand with transition characteristics of Gothic and Renaissance styles.
>
> *Lorenzetti.*

Coming down the *left aisle* of the church, we find on the wall
Giovanni Bellini: *Virgin Enthroned.*

> The painters of the Middle Ages were no more concerned about the 'real' colours of things than they were about their real shapes. In the miniatures, enamel work and panel paintings, they loved to spread out the purest and most precious colours they could get with shining gold and flawless ultramarine blue as a favourite combination. The great reformers of Florence were less interested in colour than in drawing. That does not mean, of course, that their pictures were not exquisite in colour—the contrary is true—but few of them regarded colour as one of the principal means of welding the various figures and forms of a picture into one unified pattern. They preferred to do this by means of perspective and composition before they even dipped their brushes into paint. The Venetian painters, it seems, did not think of colour as an additional adornment for the picture after it had been drawn on the panel. When one enters the little church of San Zaccaria in Venice and stands before the picture which

the great Venetian painter Giovanni Bellini had painted over the altar there in 1505 in his old age, one immediately notices that his approach to colour was very different. Not that the picture is particularly bright or shining. It is rather the mellowness and richness of the colours that impress one before one even begins to look at what the picture represents. I think that even a photograph conveys something of the warm and gilded atmosphere which fills the niche in which the Virgin sits enthroned, with the infant Jesus lifting His little hand to bless the worshippers before the altar. An angel at the foot of the altar softly plays the violin while the saints stand quietly at either side of the throne: St. Peter with his key and book, St. Catherine with the palm of martyrdom and the broken wheel. St. Apollonia and St. Jerome, the scholar who translated the Bible into Latin, and whom Bellini therefore represented as reading in a book. Many Madonnas with saints have been painted before and after, in Italy and elsewhere, but few were ever conceived with such dignity and repose. In the earlier days, the picture of the Virgin used to be rigidly flanked by the traditional images of the saints. Bellini knew how to bring life into a simple symmetrical arrangement without upsetting its order. He also knew how to turn the traditional figures of the Virgin and saints into real and living beings without divesting them of their old character and dignity. He did not even sacrifice the variety and individuality of real life, as Perugino had done to some extent. St. Catherine with her dreamy smile, and St. Jerome, the old scholar engrossed in his book, are real enough in their own ways, although they, too, no less than Perugino's figures, seem to belong to another more serene and beautiful world, a world transfused with that warm and supernatural light that fills the picture.

Gombrich.

The best J. Bellini in Venice, after that of San G. Crisostomo.
Ruskin.

Back to the Riva degli Schiavoni; to the right over the bridge— Ponte della Pietà (leaning campanile of S. Giorgio dei Greci visible on left)—to church of the Pietà.

Inside, ceiling fresco
G. B. Tiepolo: *The Triumph of Faith.*

Above entrance door (seen best from near high altar)
Moretto da Brescia: *Jesus at Simon's House.*

This grand, but sadly restored, picture was painted in 1544 for San Fermo, at Monselice, and brought to Venice in 1740. Richard Wagner was so pleased with this work that while in Venice he paid frequent visits to it. In the background is seen the artist's native city.

Hare.

(For permission to go up to the choir, ask verger.)

Continue along the Riva degli Schiavoni, over the next bridge, and left into the narrow Calle del Dose. This emerges in front of the late C15 church of S. Giovanni in Bragora.

On the high altar
Cima da Conegliano: *Baptism of Jesus.*

In the chapel to the left of the high altar, and on the right wall
Bartolomeo Vivarini: Triptych—*Virgin between John the Baptist and Saint Andrew.*

Coming down the left aisle, we find on the wall

Alvise Vivarini: *Resurrection of Jesus.*
Cima da Conegliano: *Constantine Holding the Cross.*
Alvise Vivarini: *Madonna and Child.*

Right outside the church and out of the campo immediately on the right—down Calle dei Preti or Calle Crosera; left at Calle del Pestrin, over the iron bridge to the Arsenal. It was formerly of great importance, and the basis of the Republic's sea power and trade.

Outside the main gates of the Arsenal, among a pride of peers, there stands a tall marble lion,* gangling but severe. This beast was brought from Athens in 1687 by the fighting Doge Francesco Morosini (chiefly eminent in universal history because a shell from one of his ships exploded the Turkish powder magazine that happened to be inside the Parthenon). The lion used to guard the gateway into the Piraeus, and was so celebrated among the ancients that the port itself was known as the Port of the Lion: but when it arrived at the Arsenal, booty of war, the Venetians were puzzled to discover that engraved upon its shoulders and haunches were some peculiar inscriptions, not at all Greek in

* On left of Gateway.

style, in characters that seemed to the eyes of a people accustomed to the exquisite calligraphies of Arabic, rudely and brusquely chiselled. For several centuries nobody knew what these letters were: until one nineteenth century day a visiting Danish scholar inspected them, raised his arms in exultation, and pronounced them to be Norse runes. They were carved on the lion in the eleventh century by order of Harold the Tall, a Norwegian mercenary who fought several campaigns in the Mediterranean, conquering Athens and once dethroning the Emperor in Constantinople, only to die in 1066 as King of Norway, fighting Harold the Saxon at Stamford Bridge, Yorkshire. The inscription on the lion's left shoulder says: 'Haakon, combined with Ulf, with Asmud and with Orn, conquered this port. These men and Harold the Tall imposed large fines, on account of the revolt of the Greek people. Dalk has been detained in distant lands. Egil was waging war, together with Ragnar, in Roumania and Armenia.' And on the right haunch of this queer animal is inscribed, in the runic: 'Asmund engraved these runes in combination with Asgeir, Thorleif, Thord and Ivar, by desire of Harold the Tall, although the Greeks on reflection opposed it.'

Morris.

On the right of the gateway, the middle lion brought here in C18, is Greek, C6 B.C. (head added later).

Return along Calle del Pestrin; turn right at No. 3892—Calle dei Corazzeri; left along small square, right into Salizada S. Antonin; just before bridge, right along Fondamenta dei Furlani to S. Giorgio degli Schiavoni. First floor—the series of paintings by Carpaccio. (Charge for admission.)

Starting from the left—*Scenes from the Life of Saint George*
1. *St. George killing the dragon.*
2. *Triumph of St. George.*
(After C17 panel on end wall, beside altar.)
3. *Saint George Baptising Eastern King.*
After the altar, continuing to the left—*Saint Tryphone Subdues a Demon in the Form of a Basilisk.*

On the right wall:
1. *Agony in the Garden.*

2. *The Calling of Saint Matthew.*
Carpaccio has set this incident in the Ghetto (p. 201).

114

The last three paintings are episodes from the life of Saint Jerome.
1 *Saint Jerome Leads the Tamed Lion to the Monastery.*
2. *Funeral of Saint Jerome.*
3. *Saint Jerome in his Study.* (Now believed to be Saint Augustin.)

> Carpaccio's Saint Jerome in his Cell depicts a Venetian scholar's pleasant studio rather than the austere retreat of an ascetic. The Saint, clothed in a scarlet cape and white surplice, sits writing at an elegant desk. Manuscripts in costly red bindings and musical scores lie scattered about. The sea-shell on the table attests to the fondness for curios, strange objects and bizarre natural formations which was typical of the period. Carpaccio does not omit the armillary sphere—for interest in astronomy was widespread among cultivated people—nor above all, the collector's shelves (on the left-hand wall). Here we make out the small terra cotta vases and bronze statuettes dear to the antique lovers of the time.
>
> *Chastel.*

At this point there is an *optional excursion* to the church of S. Francesco della Vigna. It is distinguished by having a façade designed by Palladio and an interior designed by Sansovino (though his design was modified during construction). To reach S. Francesco, turn left outside S. Giorgio, along the Calle dei Furlani, left at the end into Campo Foscolo: across the Campo, left along the Salizzada delle Gatte, Salizzada S. Francesco and Ramo Ponte S. Francesco. The church contains, on the entrance wall, left of entrance door:
Antonio Vivarini (attr.): *Three Saints.*

Fifth Chapel on the Right
Chapel of the Barbaro Family.

> The Cappella Barbaro was founded by Francesco Barbaro, 1480–1568, to contain the ashes of his illustrious ancestors, amidst whom he is buried himself. His tomb bears the device—a red circle ('tondo') on a field argent—which was granted in 1125 to the Admiral Marco Barbaro, in remembrance of his having, during the battle of Ascalon, cut off the hand of a Moor who had seized the flag of his vessel, slain him, and turned his turban into a banner, after having traced a red circle with his bleeding arm.
>
> *Hare.*

Chapel in Right Transept
Standing on C16 altar and surmounted by C16 addition of *Holy*

Father, altarpiece—Antonio da Negroponte: *Virgin and Child, Enthroned.*

A door in the left transept leads into a corridor. To the right, various chapels, of which the first contains a panel—Giovanni Bellini: *Virgin and Child, Saints and Donor.*

Come back to S. Giorgio the same way.

In front of S. Giorgio take the Fondamenta dei Furlani back to the bridge—the Ponte S. Antonin; then right over the bridge along the Salizzada dei Greci, take the left turn to the Greek Institute (*Istituto Ellenico*). The custodian will admit you (admission charge) to a remarkable collection of Greek icons belonging to the Greek community in Venice. They are housed in the C17 Scuola di San Nicoló designed by Longhena. Ask to see the oval staircase on the left of the entrance and the Assembly Hall on the first floor.

In the same courtyard is C16 church of S. Giorgio dei Greci. Beyond, C16 leaning Campanile (which we saw from the Ponte della Pietà) with small Renaissance loggia; beyond, a C15 well-head; beyond, a small C17 palace, the treasury of the church.

We now return towards the Piazza—over the Ponte dei Greci, along the Fondamenta dell'Osmarin into Campo S. Provolo. At the end of the Campo, on left, Gothic arch with C15 marble relief. We do not go under this arch (it leads into the Campo S. Zaccaria), but go over the Ponte S. Provolo and straight ahead to Ponte di Canonica. The Prison, Bridge of Sighs and Ducal Palace appear on the left. Go along the Fondamenta di Canonica to the point where the private bridge leads to the C16 Palazzo Trevisan (now show rooms for Venetian ceramics).

> In the inlaid design of the dove with the olive-branch of the Casa Trevisan, it is impossible for anything to go beyond the precision with which the olive leaves are cut out of the white marble; and, in some wreaths of laurels below, the rippled edge of each leaf is finely and easily drawn, as if by a delicate pencil. No Florentine table is more exquisitely finished than the façade of this entire palace; and as an ideal of executive perfection, this palace is most notable amidst the architecture of Europe.
>
> *Ruskin.*

The Ramo (Calle) di Canonica leads back to the Piazza.

The Riva degli Schiavoni engraved in 1754 by Vissentini from Canaletto's drawing may be compared with the view Canaletto did some ten years earlier (p. 56); In the middle ground can be seen the Palazzo Nani-Mocenigo. The extension of the Fondamenta beyond the Ponte di Paglia had been completed when the drawing below was done in 1843. The buildings to the left of the Danieli, which today have been replaced by an extension of the hotel, can be seen nearly one hundred years earlier in the upper illustration.

Ascension Day, 1746. The Doge Alvise Mocenigo IV departing in the state gondola, Il Bucintoro, for the Lido to conduct the annual ceremony of the marriage of the sea. This rite was initiated in the year 997 by the Doge Orseolo II.

The Doge threw a ring into the water with the words 'Ti sposiam, o mare nostro, in signo di vero e perpettuo dominio'.

The church of San Francesco della Vigna, drawn by Luca Carlevaris (1663-1731) about 1725 shows the characteristic Palladio facade on the west front which was superimposed on Jacopo Sansovino's (1486-1570) original design.

The church of San Giorgio de Greci and its campanile in 1720. The present condition of the tower can be seen in Kaffe Fasset's drawing on the facing page.

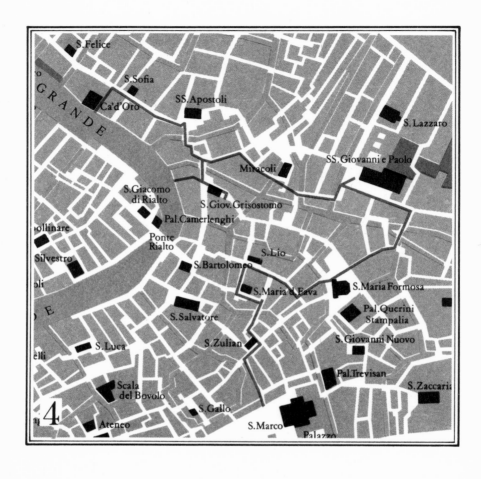

Everything around me is praiseworthy, a great, reputable work of joint human endeavour, a splendid monument, not of a master, but of a people.

Goethe.

4

San Zanipolo – Miracoli – Ca'd' Oro

Start from the Piazza; go under the clock tower into the Merceria dell'Orologio. Immediately on the left is the Sottoportego del Cappello Nero. The white stone in the pavement commemorates the spot where a brick felled the standard-bearer of Bajamonte's rebellion. The old woman who threw it is represented in a relief on the Sottoportego, crying 'Death to tyrants'. This sentiment is characteristic. The moral the Venetians drew from the overthrow of the Roman republic was that no individual should ever be permitted to acquire personal power. Even the power of Doge was strictly circumscribed. In the context of the tyrannies and despotisms of mediaeval Europe, the diffusion of power achieved by the Venetian constitution was truly remarkable, and it was nowhere paralleled (outside primitive and tribal societies) until the rise of the modern democracies.

> 'Del mille trecento e diese
> A mezzo el mese delle ceriese
> Bagiamonte passò el ponte
> E per esso fo fatto el consegio di diese'
>
> In the year thirteen hundred and ten
> In the middle of the month of the cherries
> Bajamonte crossed the bridge
> And because of that they made the Council of Ten.

Continue down the Merceria. Turn right into Ramo S. Zulian, left at the church of S. Zulian, straight through the Campo S. Zulian; the way narrows and soon the Piscina S. Zulian goes off to the right. Go through the Piscina, over the bridge, and turn left under the Sottoportego Licini; then straight on through Corte Licini and Ramo Licini, to emerge in the Campo and in front of the C18 church of Santa Maria della Fava.

First Altar on right
   G. B. Tiepolo: *Madonna and Child with Saints.*

Middle Altar on left
   Piazzetta: *Madonna and Child with Saint.*

Out of the entrance door, turn right and follow the wall of the church (Ramo della Fava) for a few yards, turn left into the Calle della Fava, which emerges into a Campo (S. Lio)—at which point, turn right into the Salizada S. Lio. Along the Salizada for some little way, then left along the Calle del Mondo Nuovo. This leads quickly to the Campo Santa Maria Formosa. It has been used for bullfights and as an open-air theatre. In this square, the church of the same name —mainly late C15. At the foot of the baroque campanile (1611)— a grotesque masque. The entrance to the church is to the right—facing the canal.

> Architecturally this interior is unique. Rebuilt by Mauro Coducci in 1492 on an earlier, probably eleventh century, plan, it is a peculiarly attractive cross between the Veneto-Byzantine and the Venetian Renaissance styles, reminding one of what the latter owed to the former. With its screens of slender columns supporting the little cupolas and barrel vaults, the interior combines the elegance of early renaissance ornament with the spatial effects of a Byzantine church.
>
> *Honour.*

> The lucid structure of this building contrasts with the interest in surface decoration which is more general in Venice: it would read more strongly if the column coverings and other ecclesiastical clutter were removed.
>
> *Litchfield.*

On the right, in the first chapel, on the altar (use the light)
   Bartolemeo Vivarini: *Triptych.*

In the right transept, on the left (i.e. the east) wall
   Palma il Vecchio: *Altarpiece—Saint Barbara.*

> An almost unique presentation of a hero-woman, standing in calm preparation for martyrdom, without the slightest air of pietism, yet with the expression of mind filled with serious conviction.
>
> *George Eliot.*

The head is of a truly typical Venetian beauty; the whole is finished with the greatest power and knowledge of colour and modelling.

Burckhardt.

The door at the end of the left transept opens out into the Campo. The various styles of Venetian palazzo are well represented around this square. Fragments of Byzantine carving (including a cross admired by Ruskin) decorate No. 5246. No. 5250 is a handsome C16 example.

The Querini Stampalia Collection is nearby; it can be regarded as an optional extra for the energetic. The way is signed from the Campo to the entrance of the Palazzo: it gives an interesting impression of a late C18 Venetian aristocrat's house (less grand than the Ca' Rezzonico—p. 172); it contains a lot of works of very minor importance, but a few are of more interest.

Room VIII (Renaissance Room)
Giovanni Bellini (attr.): *Madonna and Child Blessing.*
Giovanni Bellini: *Presentation in the Temple,* an early work, closely modelled on a work of Mantegna (of which there is a photograph behind the curtain nearby).
Mantegna: *Presentation.*
Palma Vecchio: *Portrait of Francesco Querini and Wife* (unfinished).

Room XI
Longhi: *The Sagredo Family.*

Room XII
Longhi: *The Lion's Cage* and other incidents of C18 life.

Room XIII
More small works of Longhi, including
Longhi: *Duck Shooting on the Lagoon* (so much better than the others, it is thought by Honour to be possibly the work of another artist).

From the Campo take the opening by the clock—the Calle Lunga. You will come to a bridge in front of you. Do not go over it; instead, go over the bridge on your left—the Ponte Tetta (from which are particularly charming views).

The way crosses over the Ponte dell'Ospedaleto and comes out opposite the Casa di Ricovero—the *ospedaletto* (almshouse). Inside there remains a C17 oval staircase, and on the first floor in the Music Room—a pretty little C18 room with frescoes by Jacopo Guarana.

This seldom-visited room is a complete piece of 'settecento' decoration, in which every available wall space has been frescoed and ornamented light-heartedly and intimately; only the existence of radiators there discreetly reveals that time has passed. The children of the Ospedaletto were famous for the concerts they gave, and Guarana has taken up the theme of music in a charmingly half-humorous, half-poetic Apollo with female musicians who play at one end of the oval room among painted marble columns. The whole deceptive architectural setting is the work of Agostino Mengozzi-Colonna, son of the architectural painter who had been Tiepolo's constant collaborator in such schemes. Agostino's 'trompe l'oeil' is in the best tradition of his father, while Guarana has peopled it with those vaguely classical figures in vaguely period costume, who are not taking themselves too seriously.

Part of Guarana's charm is in this unpretentiousness and even in irrelevance. The dog on the steps is sufficient to tell us that the fresco is Venetian: it has strayed out of ordinary life, to be teased by the woman at the right who extends a doughnut to it, and is a comic adjunct to Apollo earnestly conducting; and it also aids the illusionism of Mengozzi-Colonna's steps. Since Veronese, at least, there had been a cheerful Venetian tradition of irrelevance, if not irreverence in depictions of solemn scenes. Like his master Tiepolo, Guarana is not concerned with a serious classical world but with creating a piquant and impressive effect: which indeed he succeeds in doing. And Mengozzi-Colonna is concerned with creating an effect of space by a Palladian-style portico of double columns (almost like a miniature of Adam's portico for Osterley) and nothing but sky beyond. First the room is dignified by simulated architecture, its proportions enhanced by the figures, and then the wall is dissolved into the lilac space of limitless sky. Guarana and Mengozzi-Colonna thus assert, for almost the last time, that pre-occupation of their age with illusionism in decoration. . . .

Levey.

The little curved singing gallery is characteristic of the period.

The music, which, according to my taste, is far superior to that of the opera, and which has not its like, either in Italy or the rest of the world, is that of the 'scuole'. The 'scuole' are charitable institutions, founded for the education of young girls without means, who are subsequently portioned by the Republic either for marriage or for the cloister. Amongst the accomplishments

cultivated in these young girls music holds the first place. Every
Sunday, in the church of each of these 'scuole', during Vespers,
motets are performed with full chorus and full orchestra, composed and conducted by the most famous Italian masters, executed
in the latticed galleries by young girls only, all under twenty
years of age. I cannot imagine anything so voluptuous, so touching
as this music. The abundant art, the exquisite taste of the singing,
the beauty of the voices, the correctness of the execution—
everything in these delightful concerts contributes to produce an
impression which is certainly not 'good style' but against which
I doubt whether any man's heart is proof.

Rousseau.

Coming out of the Ospedaleto, Longhena's façade of the Ospedaleto
church is immediately on the right. As Wittkower remarks, the structure
seems submerged under glittering sculptural decoration.

A little farther begins the Campo San Zanipolo (Ss. Giovanni e
Paolo) — a good stop for coffee. You come first to a fine C16 well-head,
and then to the late C15 equestrian statue of Colleoni, modelled by
Verrocchio and cast by a Venetian caster. It was originally gilded.
It is regarded by Countess Volpi as the greatest equestrian statue of
the renaissance.

When the great mercenary Colleoni died in 1484, he left his
entire fortune of nearly half a million ducats to the State (which
badly needed it) on condition that a statue was erected to him in
'the Piazza before St. Mark's'. The signory gratefully accepted
the cash, but could not stomach the notion of a monument in the
great Piazza, so reached a characteristic compromise with the
truth. They commissioned the statue all right, and erected it in
a piazza before St. Mark's—but it was the 'School' of St. Mark's,
not the Basilica, and the memorial stands there still in the square
outside the San Zanipolo.

Morris.

The fine Renaissance façade of the Scuola di S. Marco stretches
from the canal to the church. It is thought that Corducci, who completed the top of the façade, intended to recall the curves of the
Basilica di S. Marco.

The church was built by Dominican friars.

From the middle of the C13 the leading tendencies in all
Continental countries were towards space in terms of uninter-
rupted breadth and plainness. These tendencies in Spain, Germany,

Italy and France, were connected chiefly with the rise of the orders of friars, the Franciscans and Dominicans (or Grey Friars and Black Friars), founded in 1209 and 1215, and spreading from 1225 onwards.

The C13 churches of the friars were all large, simple and useful, with little to suggest a specifically ecclesiastical atmosphere. They did not need much in the way of eastern chapels, as many of the friars were not priests, but they could not do without very spacious naves to house the large congregations which came to listen to their popular sermons.

The friars, it is known, were the orders of the people. They scorned the secluded and leisurely existence of the other orders on their country estates, chose busy towns to settle in and there developed their sensational preaching technique as a medium of religious propaganda to a degree never attempted since the days of the Crusades. Thus all they needed was a large auditorium, a pulpit, and an altar.

Italy built the earliest of all Franciscan churches, S. Francesco in Assisi, begun in 1228, as a vaulted aisleless room with vaulted transept and a polygonal chancel. Later the Italian Franciscans and Dominicans have aisleless halls with timber roofs and Cistercian chancels or aisled flat-roofed, or aisled vaulted building. (Saints Giovanni e Paolo, Venice, late C13; Frari, Venice, 1340.) But, whether aisled or unaisled, vaulted or unvaulted, each church is always one spatial unity, with piers (often round or polygonal) merely subdividing it. In this is shown a very important new principle. In early or High Gothic churches the nave and aisles were separate channels or parallel movements through space. Now the whole width and length of the room, thanks to the wide bays and thin supports, appears all one.

Pevsner.

On either side of the late C15 doorway, two reliefs—a C13 Byzantine *Annunciation*; on the extreme right, a marble relief, very worn—*Daniel in the Lion's Den*—perhaps C6. Inside, on the entrance wall, immediately on the right—C15 monument to Doge Giovanni Mocenigo.

Here the sad idea of death is completely banished, and the Christian remembrances are restricted in this representation, to *The Taking Down of Christ From the Cross*, to the *Saviour* and to a few *Saints*, while the classical and pagan exaltation of life is emphasized and devoted to the glorifying of the deeds and of the figure of the valiant Doge. . . .

Lorenzetti.

After first altar on right
  Bragadin Memorial.

The defence of Famagosta, the principal city in Cyprus, was
one of the most heroic exploits of the age: the combined conduct
and valour of the Venetian governor, Bragadino, were the theme
of universal praise; honourable terms were to be granted to the
garrison; and when he notified his intention to be in person the
bearer of the keys, the Turkish commander replied in the most
courteous and complimentary terms, that he should feel honoured
and gratified by receiving them. Bragadino came, attended by
the officers of his staff, dressed in his purple robes, and with a red
umbrella, the sign of his rank, held over him. In the course of the
ensuing interview the Pasha suddenly springing up, accused him
of having put some Mussulman prisoners to death: the officers
were dragged away and cut to pieces, whilst Bragadino was
reserved for the worst outrages that vindictive cruelty could
inflict. He was thrice made to bare his neck to the executioner,
whose sword was thrice lifted as if about to strike: his ears were
cut off; he was driven every morning for ten days, heavy laden
with baskets of earth, to the batteries, and compelled to kiss the
ground before the Pasha's pavilion as he passed. He was hoisted
to the yard-arm of one of the ships and exposed to the derision of
the sailors. Finally, he was carried to the square of Famagosta,
stripped, chained to a stake on the public scaffold, and slowly
flayed alive, while the Pasha looked on. His skin, stuffed with straw,
was then mounted on a cow, paraded through the streets with the
red umbrella over it, suspended at the bowsprit of the admiral's
galley, and displayed as a trophy during the whole voyage to
Constantinople. The skin was afterwards purchased of the Pasha
by the family of Bragadino, and deposited in an urn in the church
of Saints Giovanni e Paolo.

Quarterly Review No. 274.

Second Altar
  Giovanni Bellini: Altarpiece—*Episodes in the Life of S. Vincenzo*, in
central panels and predella; *Annunciation* and *Pietà*. An early work, its
modelling plainly indebted to Montegna, but its colouring very much
Bellini the Venetian. 'There is,' says one critic, 'a nostalgic enchantment
in the misty atmosphere and a Giorgione-like musical ecstasy provided
by an angel playing a viol.'

In front of the entrance to the next chapel, on the floor—C15
tombstone; just beyond, on the right wall, the *Valier Mausoleum*.

Towering from the pavement to the vaulting of the church, behold a mass of marble, sixty or seventy feet in height, of mingled yellow and white, the yellow carved into the form of an enormous curtain, with the ropes, fringes, and tassels, sustained by cherubs; in front of which, in the now usual stage attitudes, advance the statues of the Doge Bertuccio Valier, his son, the Doge Silvester Valier, and his son's wife, Elizabeth. The statues of the Doges, though mean and Polonius-like, are partly redeemed by the ducal robes; but that of the Dogaressa is a consummation of grossness, vanity, and ugliness—the figure of a large and wrinkled woman, with elaborate curls in stiff projection round her face, covered from her shoulders to her feet with ruffs, furs, lace, jewels, and embroidery. Beneath and around are scattered virtues, Victories, Fames, Genii—the entire company of the monumental stage assembled, as before a drop-scene—executed by various sculptors, and deserving attentive study as exhibiting every condition of false taste and feeble conceptions. The Victory in the centre is particularly interesting; the lion by which she is accompanied, springing on a dragon, has been intended to look terrible, but the incapable sculptor could not conceive any form of dreadfulness, could not even make the lion look angry. It looks only lachrymose;—its uplifted forepaws, there being no spring nor motion in its body, give it the appearance of a dog begging.

Ruskin.

After the Valier Mausoleum—still on the right, the early C18 chapel of San Domenico. The curving canvas overhead is Piazzetta: *Glory of S. Domenico* and early example of the aerial vision, a manner made famous by Tiepolo.
In the right transept: on the right (i.e. west) wall
Alvise Vivarini: *Jesus Bearing the Cross.*

On the end (i.e. south) wall Gothic window with C15 stained glass. Below, on the right—Lotto: *Saint Antonio Giving Alms* (use light).

Under the saint, behind a parapet hung with a Turkey carpet, are two deacons, in face and gesture so individualized and yet so typical that, in similar circumstances, you still see their like anywhere in Italy. One of them receives petitions and tries to control the crowd, while the other, with a look of compassion, is taking money out of a bag to give to the poor, who hustle up, a dozen heads producing the impression of a multitude. The deacon receiving the petitions is one of Lotto's best figures, considered both as painting and as a psychology.

The expression Titian gave to the ideals of his own age has that grandeur of form, that monumental style of composition, that arresting force of colour, which make the world recognize a work of art at once, and for ever acclaim it as classic. But with all these qualities, Titian's painting is as untinged by individuality as Bellini's. Indeed, to express the master passions of a majority implies a power of impersonal feeling and vision and implies, too, a certain happy insensibility—the very leaven of genius, perhaps.

This insensibility, this impersonal grasp of the world about him Lotto lacked. A constant wanderer over the face of Italy, he could not shut his eyes to its ruin nor make a rush for a share of the spoils. The real Renaissance, with all its blithe promise, seemed over and gone. Lotto, like many of his noble countrymen, turned to religion for consolation. But not to official Christianity of the past, nor to the stereotype Romanisms of the nearer future. His yearning was for immediate communion with God, although true to his artistic temperament, he did not reject forms made venerable by long use and sweet associations.

Christianity, it will be remembered, owed its rapid growth and final triumph in large measure to the personal relation it attempted universally to establish between Man and God. Pushed into the background while the Church was devoting itself to the task of civilizing barbarian hordes, this ideal of a close relation between God and man revived with the revival of culture, and became in the sixteenth century the aim of all religious striving. A brave Italian band trusted that they would be able to make religion personal once more without becoming Protestant. We all know of the sad failure of Contarini and Sadolet. Lotto had the same temper of mind and he remained as unappreciated as they, for Titian and Tintoretto swept him into oblivion, as Carafa and Loyola effaced the protestantizing cardinals.

Italy was tired of turmoil and was ready to pay any price for fixed conditions and settled institutions. It soon appeared that the price demanded was abject submission to the decrees of the Council of Trent, and Italy paid it without scarcely a murmur. If the Council of Trent meant anything, it meant the eradication of every personal element from Christianity. Bearing this in mind, we can see how inevitable was the failure of men like Contarini, Sadolet and Lotto—men to whom their own souls were as important as Christianity itself, who wanted more personality rather than less. But Italy was not ready to see, that personality—as they wanted it—was a very different affair from the individualism of which she was heartily weary.

Both Titian and Lotto are dramatic. Titian attains his dramatic effects by a total subordination of individuality to the strict purpose of a severe architectonic whole. The bystanders are mere

133

reflectors of the emotion which it is the purpose of the artist their presence should heighten; their personality is of no consequence. Lotto, on the other hand, attains his dramatic effect in the very opposite way. He makes us realize the full import of the event by the different feelings it inspires in people of different kinds.

Berenson.

High Altar, on left wall, finely proportioned Renaissance monument —Memorial to Doge Andrea Vendramin. The marble effigy of the sleeping Doge nicely illustrates the Venetian concern with surface rather than structure: the back side is blank.

From the church, go out of the Campo at the far left corner, along the Fondamenta Dandolo, then over the Ponte Rosso. On the next bridge, a view of the Palazzo Van Axel; right immediately after this bridge, following the way to the left and emerging in front of the Church of the Miracoli. The building is immediately charming. Part of the charm is in the surprise—the sudden approach, the un-Venetian style. But it repays contemplation: you can see the back of the church by taking the calle at the right and crossing the bridge of S. Maria Nuova.

> Santa Maria dei Miracoli, built by Pietro and Tullio Lombardo from 1481 to 1489, is the crowning work of the Lombard style. In bringing them to Venice they transposed the qualities of Milanese and Cremonese terra cotta into marble.* The colored areas are no longer merely decorative, but become basic elements of the spatial composition. . . .
>
> Carpaccio . . . and Mansueti, faithful portrayers of the subtle charms of Venetian dwellings, often reproduced the luxurious effects of these many-colored inlays. The Lombardi used them profusely in their works and they are displayed to particular advantage on the pretty façade of the Palazzo Dario (1487).†
>
> The altar screen is carved as delicately as lace, the cornice and pilasters are covered with graceful arabesques, and delightful bas-reliefs of putti and sirens ornament the base.
>
> *Chastel.*

From the Campo outside the entrance, over the bridge (Ponte dei Miracoli), along the Calle dei Miracoli·and Calle Boldu; turn left at the end along Salizada San Canciano, into the Campo Flaminio Corner, and over the bridge on the left into Campo S. Giovanni

* The types of marble used are listed by Hare as Pavonazzetto, Broccatello Rosso, Veronese, Porphyry, Verde-Antico, Alabastro-pecotrella, and Serpentino.
† p. 151.

Cristostomo. Just as you come into the Campo, you will see the very narrow Calle del Scaleter—which leads into the Campiello del Remer, on the Grand Canal. The outside staircase and windows are vestiges of a C13 palazzo.

One of the houses in the Corte del Remer is remarkable as having its great entrance on the first floor, attained by a bold flight of steps, sustained on four pointed arches wrought in brick. The rest of the aspect of the building is Byzantine, except only that the rich sculptures of its archivolt show in combats of animals, beneath the soffit, a beginning of the gothic fire and energy. The moulding of its plinth is of a gothic profile, and the windows are pointed, not with a reversed curve, but in a pure straight gable, very curiously contrasted with the delicate bending of the pieces of marble armour cut for the shoulders of each arch. There is a two-lighted window on each side of the door, sustained in the centre by a basket-worked Byzantine capital: the mode of covering the brick archivolt with marble, both in the windows and doorway, is precisely like that of the true Byzantine palaces.

Ruskin.

Return to the Campo, for the church of S. Giovanni Crisostomo. It was built by Coducci (of Scuola di S. Marco) about 1500.

The plan, a Greek cross with a central cupola was one particularly admired by Renaissance architects no less for its beautiful simplicity than its symbolism—a combination of the square and circle representing the relation between man and the universe and the cross standing for the redemption. There are two pictures of outstanding importance. Above the first altar on the right is Giovanni Bellini's *St. Jerome with St. Christopher and St. Augustine,** painted in 1513 when he was an octogenarian. The treatment of the soulful St. Christopher and the gentle hilly landscape reveal how the old artist fell under the spell of Giorgione who had died three years before; while the elegant marble pilaster in the centre, which looks like the jamb of a chimney-piece, seems to have been taken from the work of another of his younger contemporaries, Tullio Lombardo. The influence of Giorgione marks, still more strongly, Sebastiano del Piombo's *St. John Chrysostom and Six Saints* on the high altar (1508–10). Indeed, the somewhat plump St. John the Baptist and St. Liberale who stands behind him were probably laid in by Giorgione himself shortly before his death. The third great work of art in the church is the relief of *The*

* Ask for light.

136

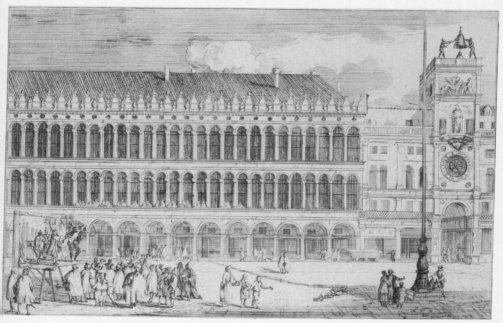

The north side of the Piazza showing much of the Procurate Vecchie and, to the right, the clock tower where walk four begins. The strolling players on their platform are dressed in the traditional Commedia de' Arte costumes.

Santa Maria Formosa in 1720, from the *Gran Teatro di Venezia*.

The Almshouse of SS Giovanni e Paolo (San Zanipolo). The early eighteenth century eye of the artist gives Longhena's somewhat heavy late baroque facade a lighter, and more rococo, look.

The church of San Zanipolo and its surroundings from the *Gran Teatro di Venezia*. West of the alms house is the statue of Colleoni standing in the campo near the church and the Scuola San Marco. At the time these plates were published the square was not paved save for a crosspath, the outline of which can be seen in the present paving. A funeral service in this church is one of the greatest honours that can be granted by the city. This privilege was recently accorded to Igor Stravinsky.

Santa Maria dei Miracoli built from 1481-1489 to a design by Pietro Lombardo (1435-1515) who was also the architect of the nearby Franciscan monastery which in this engraving by Carlevaris was still connected to the church by an overhead gallery.

The church of Santi Apostoli as it was in 1720. It was considerably remodelled later in the century (from the *Gran Teatro di Venezia*).

The Castel Forte at a canal crossing and the back of the Scuola San Rocco (from the *Gran Teatro di Venezia*) which is a characteristic building in the classical manner in Venice in the last half of the sixteenth century.

The Frari Church and its campo from the same source as the above illustration. The fourteenth century campanile is unusual for its octagonal, rather than pine-cone-shaped capping.

Until early in the eighteenth century it was the custom for the lower class members
of the rival factions, the Castellani and the Nicolotti to meet on the Ponte de Pugn

for a fist fight. This illustration of the popular spectacle from the *Gran Teatro di Venezia* is taken from an unknown earlier work of about 1700.

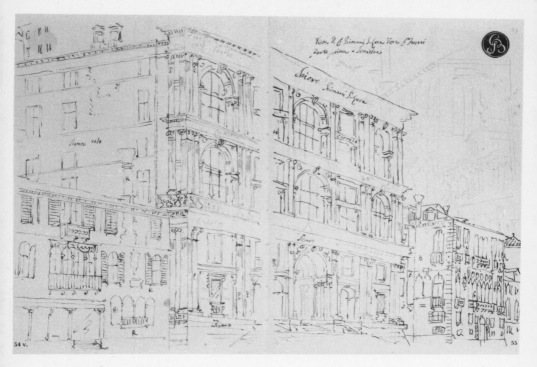

Sketch notes by Canaletto, c 1733, and Turner, 1819. Canaletto's colour notations are clearly marked on the facade, side walls and flanking palaces of the Palazzo Grimani. In 1819 Turner incorrectly identifies the campanile of San Samuele (on the right) as San Stefano and the Palazzo Rezzonico is clearly drawn on the left, but not marked.

Coronation of the Virgin, over the second altar on the left, carved between 1500 and 1502 by Tullio Lombardo who also decorated the pilasters in the chapel. With its carefully modulated rhythm of draperies and its serious self-possessed figures, this strongly classicising relief was destined to exert great influence on Venetian painters, notably Bellini and Cima.

Honour.

Behind the church, an archway leads to the Corte Prima del Milion and thence to the Corte Seconda del Milion, on the left of which is a Byzantine archway with bird and animal carvings of great beauty and assurance of style.

Back to the church and right over the bridge to the Campiello Flaminio Corner. Out of the far left corner of the Campiello—the Calle Dolfin (through the Campiello Riccardo Selvatico)—left at the canal—under the Sotoportego SS Apostoli and right on to the bridge. Behind you, above the arcade, is the façade of the Palazzo Falier.

The balcony is, of course, modern, and the series of windows has been of greater extent, once terminated by a pilaster on the left hand, as well as on the right, but the terminal arches have been walled up.

Ruskin.

At the other side of the Campo, the church of the Santi Apostoli. Internally a clean basic structure much cluttered with ecclesiastical furniture.

After first altar on right
C15 *Correr Family Chapel*, attributed to Coducci, on the altar of which (plug in light) G. B. Tiepolo: *Communion of Santa Lucia.*

Out of the Campo leads the Via Vittorio Emanuele or Strada Nova —a new street, made in the 1870's. At the beginning of this street, on the left, a handsome C18 building—the Scuola dell'Angelo Custode. Later on the left take the Calle della Ca'd'Oro. The Ca'd'Oro gives one a good impression of the surroundings in which a wealthy Venetian lived in the early C15. The Courtyard is characteristic: an open-air staircase (formerly with wooden roof), early C15 well-head in red marble. Along the walls—busts, statues, altars, columns—mostly Roman copies of Greek works.

On the first floor, a fine view of the Canal from the Loggia. To the

left of the Loggia, on the wall opposite the entrance, a C15 altar piece in thirteen panels: *Scenes of the Passion.*

The room on the left has a fine C15 wooden staircase; on a bright day you will be able to see

Paris Bordone: *Venus Asleep with Cupid, in Landscape.*

Paris Bordone: *Jesus and Saints with Angels playing Music*—c. 1500. (On staircase wall.)

On the other side of the *Portego* (central hallway), in a room with early C17 carved and gilded ceiling

Titian: *Venus* in C16 frame, believed to be a copy of his *Venus at the Mirror* (Hermitage, Leningrad).

Also early C16 *Madonna and Child with Angels.*

At the end of the Portego away from the canal, recess with carved and gilded C15 ceiling and

Mantegna: *Saint Sebastian.* On a scroll painted at the foot of the picture you can read the words: 'nil nisi divinum stabile est caetera fumus'.

In the corresponding recess on the next floor

Van Dyck: *Portrait in Black.*

Going towards the Loggia, in the last room on the right (before the Portego widens into the Loggia)

Francesco Guardi (attr.): *View of Piazzetta* and *View of Waterfront and Ponte della Salute.*

From the Loggia a door leads to a room containing a collection of bronzes.

> The bronze statuette was perhaps the most revealing of all Renaissance revivals. In this period collectors became so addicted to antique sculpture that they wished to have pieces literally to hand, pieces which they might fondle in their studies. On the whole they preferred nudes. At this time, however, Roman bronzes were hard to find and the few that had been dug up lacked the perfect finish demanded by the Renaissance connoisseur. So sculptors not unwillingly supplied the need in countless little figures of gods and mythological beings, derived from classical statues and modelled with exquisite refinement.
>
> *Honour.*

We can take the vaporetto from the ferry station outside: this is the opportunity to see the buildings on the other side of the canal—in particular the fine C18 Palazzo Correr della Regina: you will see this a little to the right, just beyond the Rio San Cassiano (the first side canal), and beside a traghetto station.

From the vaporetto, we can look back at the façade of the Ca'd'Oro.

> The left side of the Ca'd'Oro was never completed but this building remains the most typical expression of Venetian imagination, with its delicately sculptured loggias, its highly original crowning and its multicoloured facing reflected in the Grand Canal.
>
> *Chastel.*

> Ca'd'Oro represents the last flowering of the Venetian Gothic, and it is interesting to reflect that the Palazzo Medici Riccardi and Palazzo Pitti were being designed in Florence just about the time of its completion. The palace derives its name from the fact that Jean Charlier—'Zuane di Francia', a French painter—gilded the friezes, cornices and ornamental merlons in 1431.
>
> *Masson.*

> During the whole of the fifteenth century, Venice was engaged in conquering neighbouring towns, over which Venetian nobles were appointed as governors. The Republican government of Venice gave special care to the regulations for the development of trade, both in home and overseas markets. Her prosperity was due to a State commercial system, and was not the result of mere accident or of the enterprise of individuals. This successful trading community produced many kings of commerce, whose rivalry in display led to the erection of numerous fine palaces on the Grand Canal, which from their situation on the broad waterfront needed less protection against civic turmoil than was necessary in Florence and other inland cities, and so could be more splendid and open externally.
>
> . . . the extreme heat of summer was here tempered by sea breezes, and to enjoy them, belvederes and balconies were usual, these all the more necessary in that the restricted island sites gave little room for gardens. On the other hand, the northern latitude and the winds that swept down from the snow-topped mountains, made fire-places almost essential, and the funnel-topped chimneys are a distinctive Venetian feature.
>
> *Banister Fletcher.*

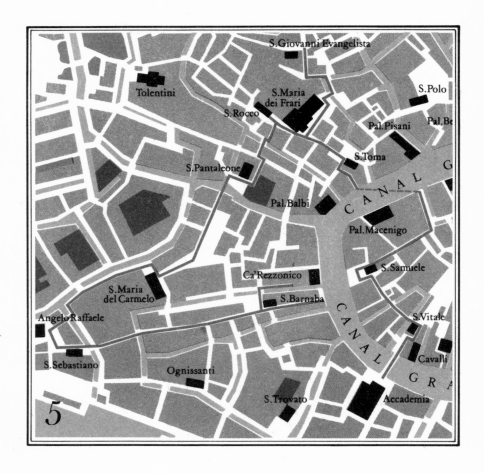

We have rediscovered the great law of town planning which radiates so delightfully through Venice.

The buildings people the sky: communications are precisely established, in cardinal roads and piazzas, with canals at another level. The pedestrian is master of the ground as he will be in the new town of our time.

Le Corbusier.

150

5

Frari – San Rocco – Carmini – Ca'Rezzonico

Go first to the Accademia Bridge (Vaporetto stop Accademia). The top of the bridge is a commanding position to view the Canal and its palazzi. Looking towards the Salute and reading the buildings from the right: first, an C18 palazzo washed ochre—the Palazzo Brandolin-Rota, where Browning stayed in 1878; next, a fine late C15 palazzo—the Palazzo Contarini del Zaffo; farther away, towards the Salute, a one-storey white building almost covered in creeper—this is the unfinished Palazzo Venier dei Leoni, which now houses the Guggenheim Collection (p. 228); farther away still, a red building, and then the Palazzo Dario. Looking the other way along the Canal, and reaching the building from the left: first, the palazzo housing the British consulate, then a C17 palazzo washed dull yellow; then the fine early C17 façade of the Palazzo Contarini; Longhena's Ca'Rezzonico closes the vista. On the opposite side of the Canal, looking left from the bridge there is first a garden and beige-coloured building, and then the elegant C17 façade (topped by pinnacles) of the Palazzo Giustiniani—an early work of Longhena.

We go over the bridge (away from the Accademia) into the Campo San Vidal: just beyond the Campo is the Church of San Vitale—now the Gallery of San Vidal (entrance on the left, at the foot of the campanile).

On the end wall of the chancel
  Carpaccio: *San Vitale on Horseback* (the horse owing much to the bronze horses of San Marco) and over, *Four Saints, Madonna and Child.*

Emerging from the gallery we turn left and left again following the wall of the church and of the house built up against the church, over the Ponte de Ca'Vitturi, and straight ahead, until we can go no farther. This is the Calle dei Orbi: turn left here, and immediately right: we come out into the Salizzada di Ca'Malipiero, with the Grand Canal on the left (Campo S. Samuele).

From here we get a good view of the façade of the Ca'Rezzonico immediately opposite: Longhena's design was carried out up to the *piano nobile* (second floor) in the C17 and makes use of the motifs from Sansovino's façade of the Library of San Marco (p. 22). The top floor was added in the mid-C18.

To the right of the Rezzonico, two small palaces, then three mid-C15 palaces all joined together, of which the first is called Palazzo Giustinian. Wagner composed the second act of *Tristan* here.

> As I was returning home late one night on the gloomy canal, the moon appeared suddenly and illuminated the marvellous palaces and the tall figure of my gondolier towering above the stern of the gondola, slowly moving his huge sweep. Suddenly he uttered a deep wail, not unlike the cry of an animal; the cry gradually gained in strength, and formed itself, after a long-drawn 'Oh!' into the simple musical exclamation 'Venezia!' This was followed by other sounds of which I have no distinct recollection, as I was so much moved at the time. Such were the impressions that to me appeared the most characteristic of Venice during my stay there, and they remained with me until the completion of the second act of *Tristan,* and possibly even suggested to me the long-drawn wail of the shepherd's horn at the beginning of the third act.
>
> *Wagner.*

With our back to the Canal, we leave the Campo on the left (Calle de la Carozze), past the church of S. Samuele Profeta on the right to the Piscina S. Samuele, at which point, we turn left and fork left down the Calle del Tragheto to the traghetto station.

On the opposite side of the canal, on the far left is the Palazzo Foscari (the last of the three palaces joined together, which we saw from S. Samuele); to the right of it, the Palazzo Balbi, topped by pinnacles, a late C16 building fore-shadowing the development of the baroque. Far to the right, another pinnacled palazzo, with fine C16 façade—the Palazzo Papadopoli.

We take the traghetto to the other side. Looking back at the buildings lining the Canal, we can just see on the left the façade of the handsome early C16 Palazzo Grimani, now the Court of Appeal, rising above the roof level of the other buildings. The last palace fully visible on the right is the Palazzo Contarini delle Figure.

> In the intervals of the windows of the first story, certain shields and torches are attached, in the form of trophies, to the stems of

two trees whose boughs have been cut off, and only one or two of their faded leaves left, scarcely observable, but delicately sculptured here and there, beneath the insertions of the severed boughs. It is as if the workman had intended to leave us an image of the expiring naturalism of the gothic school.

Ruskin.

To the left of it are four palaces joined together—the Case dei Mocenigo, in which Byron wrote *Beppo*.

> I love the language, that soft bastard Latin
> Which melts like kisses from a female mouth,
> And sounds as if it should be writ on satin,
> With syllables which breathe of the sweet South,
> And gentle liquids gliding all so pat in,
> That not a single accent seems uncouth,
> Like our harsh northern whistling, grunting gutteral,
> Which we're obliged to hiss, and spit and sputter all.
>
> I like the women too (forgive my folly),
> From the rich peasant cheek of ruddy bronze,
> And large black eyes that flash on you a volley
> Of rays that say a thousand things at once,
> To the high Dama's brow, more melancholy,
> But clear, and with a wild and liquid glance,
> Heart on her lips, and soul within her eyes,
> Soft as her clime, and sunny as her skies.

Byron: Beppo.

From the traghetto stop, follow the arrows marked 'Scuola di San Rocco' until you come out into the Campo dei Frari. Turn right, and the entrance to the church is on the left.

We enter through the Emiliani chapel; immediately on the right—the Pesaro Altar, on which Titian: *Pesaro Madonna.*

> On the left, behind the kneeling militant bishop Jacopo Pesaro, a harnessed warrior, his features probably those of Titian, has brought Turkish prisoners and raises his master's banner triumphantly. The impetus animating these figures is carried into the composition of the picture as a whole and supports the group around the Virgin. In this way the painter created here in 1519 to 1526 the first great example of a powerfully dynamic diagonal composition which was to become the prototype for Baroque painting as a whole.

Decker.

It was almost unheard of to move the Holy Virgin out of the centre of the picture, and place the two administering saints— St. Francis, who is recognizable by the Stigmate, and St. Peter, who has deposited the key on the steps of the Virgin's throne—not symmetrically on each side, as Giovanni Bellini had done, but as active participants of a scene. In this altar-piece, Titian had to revive the tradition of donors' portraits, but did it in an entirely novel way. The picture was intended as a token of thanksgiving for a victory over the Turks by the Venetian nobleman Jacopo Pesaro, and Titian portrayed him kneeling before the Virgin while an armoured standard-bearer drags a Turkish prisoner behind him. St. Peter and the Virgin look down on him benignly while St. Francis, on the other side, draws the attention of the Christ-child to the other members of the Pesaro family, who are kneeling in the corners of the picture. The whole scene seems to take place in an open courtyard, with two giant columns which rise into the clouds where two little angels are engaged in playfully raising the Cross. Titian's contemporaries may well have been amazed at the audacity with which he had dared to upset the old-established rules of composition. They must have expected, at first, to find such a picture lopsided and unbalanced. Actually it is the opposite. The unexpected composition only serves to make it gay and lively without upsetting the harmony of it all. The main reason is the way in which Titian contrived to let light, air and colours unify the scene. The idea of letting a mere flag counter-balance the figure of the Holy Virgin would probably have shocked an earlier generation, but this flag in its rich warm colour, is such a stupendous piece of painting that the venture was a complete success.

Gombrich.

The neighbouring tomb of Canova,* with its pyramidical super-structure and its suggestive half-open door, was designed by Canova—not for himself, but for Titian, who had his own plans for a truly Titianesque tomb, but died too soon to build it (he is buried in the Frari anyway in the grandest mausoleum of all† erected 300 years after his death by the Emperor of Austria, and surrounded by reliefs from his own works). In the same church‡ the fine statue of St. Jerome by Alessandro Vittoria, with its beautifully modelled veins and muscles, really portrays Titian in his old age.

Morris.

* Next but one to the left. † Opposite Canova pyramid.
‡ Opposite the Pesaro altar.

To the left, framing the side door, huge C17 monument to Doge Pesaro, with caryatids; to the left of it, neo-classic mausoleum in pyramid shape planned by Canova for Titian, but actually executed as a tomb for Canova by his pupils.

In the middle of the church, fine Choir: the work is almost entirely C15, and has both Gothic and Renaissance elements. In the main chapel, on the high altar,

Titian: *Assumption*.

Everything has been said about the mighty painters, and it is of little importance that a pilgrim the more has found them to his taste. 'Went this morning to the Academy*; was very much pleased with Titian's Assumption'.

That honest phrase has doubtless been written in many a traveller's diary, and was not indiscreet on the part of its author. But it appeals little to the general reader, and we must moreover notoriously not expose our deepest feeling. Since I have mentioned Titian's 'Assumption' I must say that there are some people who have been less pleased with it than the observer we have just imagined. It is one of the possible disappointments of Venice, and you may if you like take advantage of your privilege of not caring for it.

Henry James.

. . . the Grand Manner is an attitude rather than a style (it is, indeed, common to many examples of the High Renaissance style and nearly all that of the Baroque). The chief aim of artists using it is not to hold the mirror up to Nature. Nature should be carefully studied, at least at the outset, as providing the raw materials, but hardly more than this. The general aim is to transcend Nature, and to this end both the subject and the characters must be suitable. The subject must itself be on an elevated and elevating plane and should, if possible, be a highly memorable event. Scenes from everyday life, as such, can have no place in the repertory of the Grand Manner. Similarly, the individual figures in such a scene must be shown purged of the grosser elements of ordinary existence. In both cases the chief means of achieving this end lies in the avoidance of what is merely incidental. Landscape backgrounds or ornamental detail must be reduced to a minimum and individual peculiarities of human physiognomy absolutely eliminated. Draperies should be simple, but ample and noble, and fashionable, contemporary costume absolutely shunned. Alternatively; the figures should be nude.

* It used to be kept there.

In the latter case the musculature should be generalised and no single features stressed unduly.

. . . For the movement, drama and impetuosity shown in the 'Assunta' (finished in 1518) were utterly revolutionary and unparalleled in the placid art of Venice. The vast picture (more than 20 feet high) stands behind the high altar of the Frari. Lifting one's eyes to it one's attention is first caught by the projecting leg of the Apostle towards the right, then led up, through his body and his left arm (the latter's importance as connecting the two lower zones is stressed by being echoed in the body of the cherub which hangs down farther to the right) to the zone of the Madonna, led spirally through her body up to Christ (or God the Father) and then directed by His downward glance back to the central figure, magnificently human in itself, sublime in its situation. This main movement—into the picture and upwards—is greatly stressed at its beginnings in the lower tier, for here it has to contend with, and to dominate, every variety of contrary and subordinate movement, as if symbolizing the confusion of earthly affairs. But in the middle zone the bodies of the cherubim are completely dovetailed and absolute harmony prevails.

Gould.

On the left wall of the main chapel is the handsome late C15 Monument to Doge Nicolo Tron. The chapel to the right of the main chapel contains the Altar of the Florentines: in the central niche of the altar piece,

Donatello: *John the Baptist,* statue in painted wood.

(There is a light switch behind the pillar at the left of the entrance to the chapel.)

In the next chapel on the right, and on the left wall—a funeral memorial.

An early fourteenth century or perhaps late thirteenth century tomb, an exquisite example of the perfect gothic form. It is a knight's; but there is no inscription upon it, and his name is unknown. It consists of a sarcophagus, raised against the chapel wall, bearing the recumbent figure, protected by a simple canopy in the form of a pointed arch, pinnacled by the knight's crest; beneath which the shadowy space is painted dark blue and strewn with stars. The statue itself is rudely carved; but its lines, as seen from the intended distance, are both tender and masterly. The knight is laid in his mail, only the hands and face being bare. The hauberd and helmet are of chain-mail, the armour for the limbs of jointed steel; a tunic, fitting close to the breast, and marking the

156

157

swell of it by the narrow embroidered lines, is worn over the mail; his dagger is at his right side; his long cross-belted sword, not seen by the spectator from below, at his feet. His feet rest on a hound (the hound being his crest), which looks up towards its master. The face is turned away from the spectator towards the depth of the arch; for there, just above the warrior's breast, is carved a small image of S. Joseph bearing the infant Christ, who looks down upon the resting figure; and to this image its countenance is turned. The appearance of the entire tomb is as if the warrior had seen the vision of Christ in his dying moments, and had fallen back peacefully upon his pillow, with his eyes still turned to it, and his hands clasped in prayer.

Ruskin.

At the far end of the right transept, the door leads into the Sacristy, in the apse at the end of which,
Giovanni Bellini: Triptych: *Madonna and Child with Saints.*

The triptych is still set in its original frame, which, as Honour notes, continues the architecture of the picture. Symmetrically about the axis of the picture are set the various figures—Saints Nicholas and Peter on the left and Benedict and Mark on the right, as well as the cherubs. Despite some remaining Byzantine influences (note the tapered hands of the Madonna), 'human sweetness and soft colour', as Fiocco remarks, expel the last traces of the Byzantine inflexibility which characterised the 'San Giobbe' Altarpiece.*

We come out of the church into the Campo. It is a convenient spot for coffee.

Follow the arrow to the Scuola di S. Rocco. This early C16 building is famous for its series of vast paintings by Tintoretto. The *Crucifixion* is to be found by going through the hall on the upper floor. The works on the staircase and on the easels are mostly not Tintoretto. The *Annunciation* on an easel beside the altar upstairs is by Titian.

> Tintoretto's adolescence fell in a period when Spain was rapidly making herself mistress of Italy. The haunting sense of powers almost irresistible gave a terrible fascination to Michaelangelo's works, which are swayed by that sense as by a demonic presence. Tintoretto felt this fascination because he was in sympathy with the spirit which took form in the colossal torsoes and limbs. . . .

* Now in the Accademia, Room II, No. 38 (see p. 85).

Tintoretto had to an even greater degree the feeling that whatever existed was for mankind and with reference to man. In his youth people were once more turning to religion, and in Venice poetry was making its way more than it had previously done, not only because Venice had become the refuge of men of letters, but also because of the diffusion of printed books. Tintoretto took to the new feeling for religion and poetry as to his birthright. Yet whether classic fable or biblical episode were the subject of his art, Tintoretto coloured it with his feeling for the human life at the heart of the story. His sense of power did not express itself in colossal nudes so much as in the immense energy, in the glowing health of the figures he painted, and more still in his effects of light, which he rendered as if he had it in his hands to brighten or darken the heavens at will and subdue them to his own moods. . . .

It was a great mastery of light and shadow which enabled Tintoretto to put into his pictures all the poetry there was in his soul without once tempting us to think that he might have found better expression in words. The poetry which quickens most of his works in the Scuola di San Rocco is almost entirely a matter of light and colour. What is it but the light that changes the solitudes in which the Magdalen and St. Mary of Egypt are sitting,* into dreamlands seen by poets in their moments of happiest inspiration? What again but light and colour, the gloom and chill of evening, with the white-stoled figure standing resignedly before the judge, that give 'Christ before Pilate',† its sublime magic? What, again, but light, colour and the star-procession of cherubs that imbue the realism of the 'Annunciation'‡ with music which thrills us through and through? . . .

Christ and the Apostles, the Patriarchs and prophets, were the embodiment of living principles and of living ideals. Tintoretto felt this so vividly that he could not think of them otherwise than as people of his own kind, living under conditions easily intelligible to himself and his fellow-men. Indeed, the more intelligible and the more familiar the look and the garb and surroundings of biblical and saintly personages, the more would they drive home the principles and ideas they incarnated. So Tintoretto did not hesitate to turn every biblical episode into a picture of what the scene would look like had it taken place under his own eyes, nor to tinge it with his own mood.

Berenson.

The feeling for reality which made the great painters look upon a picture as the representation of a cubic content of atmosphere

* On either side of the altar, ground floor.   † Upstairs, small hall.
‡ Downstairs, entrance end.

enveloping all the objects depicted, made them also consider the fact that the given quantity of atmosphere is sure to contain other objects than those the artist wants for his purpose. He is free to leave them out, of course, but in so far as he does, so far is he from producing an effect of reality. The eye does not see everything, but all the eye would naturally see along with the principal objects, must be painted, or the picture will not look true to life. This incorporation of small episodes running parallel with the subject rather than forming part of it, is one of the chief character- istics of modern as distinguished from ancient art. It is this which makes the Elizabethan drama so different from the Greek. It is this again which already separates the works of Duccio and Giotto from the plastic arts of Antiquity. Painting lends itself willingly to the consideration of minor episodes, and for that reason is almost as well fitted to be in touch with modern life as the novel itself. Such a treatment saves a picture from looking prepared and cold, just as light and atmosphere save it from rigidity and crudeness.

No better illustration of this can be found among Italian masters than Tintoretto's 'Crucifixion' in the Scuola di San Rocco. The scene is a vast one, and although Christ is on the Cross, life does not stop. To most people gathered there, what takes place is no more than a common execution. Many of them are attending to it as to a tedious duty. Others work away at some menial task more or less connected with the Crucifixion, as unconcerned as cobblers humming over their last. Most of the people in the huge canvas are represented as no doubt they were in life, without much personal feeling about Christ. His own friends are painted with all their grief and despair, but the others are allowed to feel as they please.

Berenson.

Tintoret here, as in all other cases, penetrating into the root and deep places of his subject, despising all outward and bodily appearances of pain, and seeking for some means of expressing, not the rack of nerve or sinew, but the fainting of the deserted Son of God before His Eloi cry; and yet feeling himself utterly unequal to the expression of this by the countenance, has, on the other hand, filled his picture with such various and impetuous muscular exertion, that the body of the Crucified is, by comparison, in perfect repose, and, on the other, has cast the countenance altogether into shade. But the agony is told by this, and by this only: that though there yet remains a chasm of light on the mountain horizon, where the earthquake darkness closes upon the day, the broad and sunlight glory about the head of the Redeemer has become wan, *and of the colour of ashes*.

But the great painter felt he had something more to do yet.

160

A mid-seventeenth century facade in the grand manner by Giussepe Sardi fronts
the sixteenth century church of San Salvatore. The original was the combined
work of several earlier architects. On the right is the Scuolo di S. Teodoro with its
fine seventeenth century facade, also the work of Sardi, subsequently to become a
cinema.

One of the largest and busiest of Venetian squares, the Campo Santo Stefano was
until the earliest years of the nineteenth century the scene of bear baiting and
bull fighting (*Gran Teatro di Venezia*).

Veuë du pont de Realte de Venize jnuenté par Michel Ange.

Graué par Israel silueftre.   P. Mariette ex. Auec priuil. du Roy.

The segmental arch bridge known in China since the seventh century did not appear in Europe until after the return of Marco Polo, and then it was in the form of the Ponte Vecchio in Florence. Da Ponte's design was obviously based on the earlier model. Michelangelo (to whom the design is wrongly attributed in Israel Sylvestri's engraving of 1661) Sansovino, Palladio and Scamozzi all produced plans which were never adopted. The lower left illustration of the west façade (*Gran Teatro di Venezia* for this and the remaining two) is a nearly identical view of the earlier print. The Palazzo Camerlinghi occupies the centre of the upper right picture to the right of the east façade of the bridge and can be seen in all four pictures.

Giovanni Castellozzi drew the staircase of the Palazzo Contarini del Bovolo in 1721. Reached by a small alleyway off the campo Manin, this courtyard is one of Venice's most famous 'secret' places.

Not only that agony of the Crucified, but the tumult of the people, that rage which invoked His blood upon them and their children. Not only the brutality of the soldier, the apathy of the centurion, nor any other merely instrumental cause of the Divine suffering, but the fury of His own people, the noise against Him of those for whom He died, were to be set before the eye of the understanding, if the power of the picture was to be complete. This rage, be it remembered, was one of disappointed pride; and disappointment dated essentially from the time when, but five days before the King of Zion came, and was received with hosannahs, riding upon an ass, and a colt the foal of an ass. To this time, then it was necessary to divert the thought, for therein are found both the cause and the character, the excitement of, and the witness against, this madness of the people. In the shadow behind the cross, a man, riding on an ass's colt, looks back to the multitude while he points with a rod to the Christ crucified. The ass is feeding on the remnants of withered palm-leaves.

Ruskin.

To Tintoretto, lighting is the key to the emotional effect created by his pictures. We know from the early sources how much trouble he took with it, making small wax figures and disposing them in different attitudes under artificial light. And indeed the lighting with him seems almost always artificial or supernatural. The lucid light of the Italian sun, such as Bellini and the young Titian had revelled in, says nothing to his tortured and agitated mentality which, like the Northern artists with whom he had so much in common spiritually, seems most at home in highly abnormal states of illumination, in magical, phosphorescent lights, lurid storms, in every sort of weird glimmer or forests lit by glow worms. Parallels between his art and that of the Middle Ages (which was already recalled in the work of some of Mannerists) spring readily to mind, and of the medieval works easily accessible to Tintoretto, one in particular, the mosaics of S. Marco, may be relevant in this context.

They would have said little enough to the painters of the *quattrocento* and nothing at all to those of the High Renaissance, but it is in every way understandable that Tintoretto, with his romantic and anti-classical point of view, would have appreciated them. Whether or not it is legitimate to trace, as certain writers tried to do, actual formal influence from them in Tintoretto's pictures, it is at least very possible that the way in which their curved surfaces throw back occasional beams from candles with magical effect may have affected his highly peculiar lighting.

In the *Agony in the Garden** there is a mysterious glimmer every-where and other elements seem decidedly mediaeval in principle, For example, the foliage appears to be symbolic, or microcosmic: a few very large and very clearly defined leaves do duty for a whole hedge. Then again, in space composition Tintoretto is here more blatant in his disregard alike of classical prototype and even of physical possibility than ever before. Christ is suspended on no visible foundations and the mysterious procession of soldiers (violently juxtaposed in discordant scale with the Apostles) emerges from under the very ground where He sleeps. So symbolic and irrational a treatment of space had not been seen since the Middle Ages.

Gould.

At this point, the energetic may make a small excursion. Across the bridge in front of the Frari, left over Ponte San Stin, left again and immediately right (the way is signed 'Piazzale Roma'). On the left, we come to the courtyard of the Scuola di San Giovanni Evangelista.

. . . a masterpiece of Venetian Renaissance architecture—an exquisite composition of grey and white marble, stone, brick and stucco, and as Ruskin remarked 'the most characteristic example in Venice of the architecture that Carpaccio, Cima and John Bellini loved'. Yet this apparently harmonious courtyard is in fact the work of several different periods and architects.

Honour.

We return to the Frari the way we came, enter the Campo San Rocco and take the passage on the left. (It is on the right coming from the Scuola di San Rocco.) The passage leads under the Sotoportego Campiello S. Rocco (in the Campiello, picturesque view behind). Over the bridge, under the next passageway, right and immediately left down the Calle S. Pantalone; but before emerging into the next campo, turn left into the Campiello de Ca'Angaran. On the wall is a C9 or C10 Byzantine medallion, of an Eastern Emperor. Into the Campo—the Church of S. Pantalone on the right. The elaborate late C17 painted ceiling foreshadows Tiepolo. The second chapel on the right is the Chapel of S. Pantalone: behind the altar,
Veronese: *S. Pantalone Healing a Youth.*

In two or three altarpieces painted during the 'eighties (he died in 1588) Veronese shows real feeling and permits a deeper range of his emotions to enter his art than before. At the same time the

* Upstairs, large hall.

166

colours become darker and the handling more summary. What seems to be happening is that he was at last becoming affected by the atmosphere of religious urgency to which other painters had been reaching for decades. Tintoretto's example, undoubtedly, had something to do with it and this raises a very interesting point. For in his youth, as has been mentioned, Veronese had toyed with the externals of Mannerism. Now he seems veering towards the more typically Venetian form which Tintoretto exemplified to an extreme degree. He was, of course, too much of a humanist to follow it very far. But just as his work hitherto had always been behind the times, so these paintings of the 'eighties would seem to correspond with the concessions made by Titian to the spirit of the age in pictures such as the *Ecce Homo*, of the early 'forties, and in these works Veronese appears at long last to be adopting something of Titian's technique of that period.

The altarpiece of *S. Pantalone Healing a Youth* dated from 1587, the year before Veronese's death. Its effect as a whole is still far less fantastic than any altarpiece of Tintoretto. The scene is recognizably in a small back courtyard, the illumination is not mysterious—indeed, it is not stressed in any way—and the three main figures are clearly real—the group of the unconscious youth on the left and the old man anxiously supporting him is in fact touchingly human. At the same time the figure of the Saint is imbued with more than human authority and dominates the picture spiritually and physically for reasons which are not at first apparent. The chief means, in fact, by which this is achieved would seem to lie in the strange liberties taken with the space composition. The low view-point excludes the Saint's feet, those of the old man, and those of the Page. The Saint towers over us, rising from no apparent source, and what we feel is his presence. Veronese has, in fact, denied the existence of space as Tintoretto did in his *Entombment** and for the same reason. We cannot say exactly how this development would have shaped had Veronese been granted another ten years of life, but we may well believe that he might have ended his strange career as a typical Counter-Reformation painter.

Gould.

Go to the Chancel, and thence to the Little Chapel of the Sacred Nail. On the right wall,

Giovanni d'Alemagna and Antonio Vivarini: *Coronation of the Virgin* (C15).

Leaving the Church, over the bridge, the way leads us into the Campo Santa Margherita (the church on the left is now a cinema),

at the far end of which is the late C17 Scuola dei Carmini—the entrance on the right. In the upper hall, in the middle of the ceiling,
  G. B. Tiepolo: *Madonna of Mount Carmel.*

> . . . The scene which he specifically illustrates here was a vital moment in the history of the Carmelite order. The Virgin is said to have appeared on this occasion to S. Simon at Cambridge, though that detail has clearly not bothered Tiepolo. The scapular, two pieces of cloth joined by strings, is the means of obtaining an important indulgence according to a Papal Bull which is perhaps a forgery, but which Tiepolo accepts: those who have worn the scapular will be liberated from Purgatory through the Madonna's intercession on the first Saturday after their death 'or as soon as possible'.
>
> The comforting doctrine of this statement is carefully expressed in the painting. Purgatory lies all about S. Simon, and the litter of tombstones, skulls, and cloudy horrors of yawning graves contrast with the tall white figure of the Madonna triumphantly wielding aloft the Child and swept through the sky by attendant angels. The vision is almost a hallucination, and the figures of it are heightened beyond normality. We feel, and share, the Saint's privilege as he crouches low before the air-borne apparitions; like him we seem annihilated before this infraction of Nature's order.
>
> The picture certainly is part of belief, shared by Tiepolo no doubt as strongly as he shared belief in Christ's sufferings and Christ as Son of God. Indeed, so pleased were the confraternity by his work that he was made a member of it, and could thus **partake of its posthumous advantages. The S. Alvise picture***
> presents a quite unmiraculous moment: when God was suffering as a man, unaided by his divinity. But Tiepolo's mind is instinctively on the side of divinity, excited by triumphs, apotheoses and glories; he magnifies the whole conception of the Carmelite vision to his own more splendid dimensions whereby Cambridge sinks into being a Palladian-style cornice but heaven becomes a great space swept by agitated, graceful, feminine forms. In this world of celestial servants it is not the Madonna who holds the sacred scapular; the office is delegated to an angel who carries it in one hand while supporting the Madonna's draperies with another.
>
> *Levey.*

Out of the Scuola, the door into the C14 Chiesa dei Carmini faces you on the right. On the Altar immediately on the left,
  Lotto: *Saint Nicholas of Bari.*

* Visited on Excursion 7, p. 201.

What was Lotto's relation to Titian at this time? We have not a word in any contemporary writer or document to answer this question, but the *Carmini* altarpiece reveals clearly enough that *Lotto*, if not in personal relations with Titian, had at least studied his pictures, and been stung by them to emulation.

Whatever the nature of the contact, whether personal, as it scarcely could have helped being, or not, its result was the Carmini altarpiece, a work in which the qualities of composition and line, in which the conception and the feeling are to the highest degree characteristic of *Lotto*, himself, but wherein the vehicle and the colour-scheme tend to be Titianesque. The medium must have been—in so far as the present state* of the picture permits us to judge—a more fluid one and the colouring more what is called 'Venetian'—that is to say, ruddier, richer, and more fiery—than was usual with Lotto. Ludovico Dolce, a hack writer of some talent, and a parasite of the log-rolling company of which Titian, Sansovino, and Aretino were the chief partners, took occasion in his '*Dialogue on Painting*' to find fault with *Lotto's Carmini* altarpiece for its too fiery colouring. No-one today would be tempted to find fault with it on this score, and it is more than questionable whether such an objection could ever have been made in good faith. It is possible that Dolce's censure was nothing but an echo of Titian's fear of being equalled on his own ground.

Lotto's picture, far from being too fiery, does not attain the glow of Titian's masterpieces, but has instead a more than Titianesque subtlety in the juxtaposition and fusion of the colours. In few other works has Lotto created types so strong and beautiful, and seldom has his drawing been so firm, his modelling so plastic, and his colouring so glowing and harmonious. The landscape is one of the most captivating in Italian painting. The sweep of its outlines, the harmony of its colours, and the suggestiveness of its lights make an unwonted appeal to the imagination.

Berenson.

On the opposite wall (i.e. in the right aisle) on the second altar, Cima da Conegliano: *Nativity*.

Leaving the Church by the west door, we come into the Campo. We go out of the Campo by the canal, along the Fondamenta del Socorso. At the point where the way turns left, we see on the opposite bank, a brick palazzo—the Palazzo Ariani.

Palazzo Ariani, built during the 14th Century, represents in Venice the more or less well-preserved example of an elaborate open-work Loggia, a *pergola a traforo*, with loosely traceried

* It was restored in 1953.

archings. These ornamental forms, repeated and augmented, and in particular the keel arches over the side windows, appear to go back to prototypes of oriental palace architecture.

Decker.

Follow the way to the left, and take the first bridge on the right (Ponte de la Maddalena) to the Church of the Angelo Raffaele. On the entrance wall is an organ, and on the parapet is a group of paintings by Francesco Guardi (1712–1793) which have also been attributed to Gian Antonio Guardi (1698–1760).

There seems to be no 18th Century records of this series of small pictures *in situ*. They are not mentioned in the list drawn up in 1773 by the younger Zanetti (then Public Inspector of Pictures at Venice) of works of art at Angelo Raffaele; and this has suggested that they therefore date from after that year, so removing the possibility of Gian Antonio's authorship. It is hard to see why Zanetti did not mention them if they were in the church, unless he took them as merely part of the decoration of the organ case and too insignificant to need comment. If so, there is irony in the fact that he, who had lived long enough to see the complete evolution of the rococo style, did not glance at one of its final manifestations. In the Angelo Raffaele series there is the same extremeness as was appearing in France (possibly at the same time), in the work of Fragonard. The prettiness of them is almost a boudoir prettiness; the last vestiges of 17th Century solidity and prosaicism disappear and, beside Piazzetta, Guardi seems as incongruous as a butterfly against a bull.

If the series really dates from late in the century, this would make admirable sense as the last phase in Venice of that desire for air and light which Ricci had largely initiated. But the progress had never been logical or neat; and the Guardi perhaps adumbrated a final phase long before the calendar and historical neatness required. Yet from such an extreme, a return to order was inevitable. All over Europe the last exaggerated elegancies of the style were to be nipped by the colder and more correct standards of the neo-classic; everything that had been set in such quivering motion froze into marble attitudes, and beauty was sought in repose.

Levey.

Coming out of the Church, leave the Campo (Campo Drio el Cimitero) at far right corner: the campanile of S. Sebastiano (San Bastian) is immediately visible. The church contains some fine works of Veronese, which are best seen in the order in which they were painted.

First Altar on right
Veronese: *Madonna and Child with Friar*—an early work.

Sacristy (Through door under the organ), a room with C16 panelling on the ceiling
Veronese (1555): *Coronation of the Virgin* (centre); *Evangelists* (in four surrounding panels).

Ceiling of the Church
Veronese (1556): *Events in the Life of Esther.*

High Altar
Veronese (1559–61): *Madonna and Saints.*

> A composition full of vigorous, spirited figures, in which the central ones are two young men leaving some splendid dwelling, on the steps of which stands the mother, pleading and remonstrating—a marvellous figure of an old woman with a bare neck.
> *George Eliot.*

The Doors of the Organ
Veronese (c. 1561): *Presentation in the Temple* (outside); *Pool of Bethesda* (inside).

The Main Chapel
Veronese (1565): *Scenes From the Life of Saint Sebastian.*

Take the bridge outside the Church; the Calle Lunga leads straight to San Barnaba.

> The eighteenth century had the strength which comes from great self-confidence and profound satisfaction with one's surroundings. It was so self-satisfied that it could not dream of striving to be much better than it was. Everything was just right; there seemed to be no great issues, no problems arising that human intelligence untrammelled by superstition could not instantly solve. Everybody was, therefore, in holiday mood, and the gaiety and frivolity of the century were of almost as much account as its politics and culture. There was no room for great distinctions. Hair-dressers and tailors found as much consideration as philosophers and statesmen at a lady's levee. People were delighted with their own occupations, their whole lives; and whatever people delight in, that they will have represented in art. The love for pictures was by no means dead in Venice, and Longhi painted for the picture-loving Venetians their own lives

in all their ordinary domestic and fashionable phases. In the hair-dressing scenes we hear the gossip of the periwigged barber; in the dressmaking scenes, the chatter of the maid: in the dancing school, the pleasant music of the violin. There is no tragic note anywhere. Everybody dresses, dances, makes bows, takes coffee, as if there was nothing else in the world that wanted doing. A tone of high courtesy, of great refinement, coupled with all-pervading cheerfulness, distinguishes Longhi's pictures from the works of Hogarth, at once so brutal and so full of presage of change.

Berenson.

A canal runs beside the Campo; it is crossed by the Ponte dei Pugni.

On account of the cheapness of rents, this was the centre around which Venetian nobles collected who were ruined by extravagance in the eighteenth century, obtaining hence the name of Barnabotti. They claimed support from the State, and especial privileges of begging were accorded to their daughters; nevertheless they retained their votes at the Great Council, and sometimes sold them.

Hare.

From the C14–C18 this bridge—which had no balustrading in those days—was the scene of violent fights between rival factions: marks of feet are set in white stone into the surface. We go over the bridge and turn right, down the Fondamenta to the Ca'Rezzonico (the façade of which is visible from the Accademia Bridge—p. 84). It has been restored and refurnished and gives a fresh and charming impression of an C18 Venetian Palace.

We go up the grand staircase, into the huge ballroom and then (through the door on the right) into the Room of the Allegory of Marriage—the G. B. Tiepolo fresco of the *Allegory* is on the ceiling. It is part of the wit of Tiepolo's rococco manner that the irrational suspension of his encumbered chariots should be almost, but not quite, convincing.

Go down the little staircase. On the right is the room where Browning lived. Go through the China Drawing Room and the Green Lacquer Drawing Room to the delightful Yellow Drawing Room, in which,

Longhi: *The Cup of Chocolate; The Lady's Toilet.*

Back up the stairs, to the Pastels Room and thence to the Tapestries Room, with interesting furniture and three fine C17 Flemish tapestries depicting incidents in the lives of Solomon and the Queen of Sheba.

In the next room—the Throne Room, gorgeous door curtains and other furnishings, and on the ceiling,
   G. B. Tiepolo: *Merit, between Nobility and Virtue.*

Cross the *portego*: on the other side, the room nearest the Canal is the Tiepolo Room; on the ceiling,
   G. B. Tiepolo: *Fortitude and Wisdom.*

Pictures on the walls,
   Giandomenico Tiepolo: *4 Fanciful Heads of Old Men.*

The rooms on the next floor are of a more intimate and domestic character. From the top of the stairs, the opening across the *portego* and somewhat to the right leads to the Guardi Room (three frescoes attributed to Francesco Guardi); out of this (continuing rightwards) we see the Alcove Room, with its C18 painted bed. Back through the Guardi Room, we come to the Green Lacquer Room, beyond which is the Longhi Room: it contains 34 pictures by and after Longhi, among which,
Longhi: *The Rhinoceros.*

> He records thus the various animals brought to Venice at carnival times, perhaps the most exciting of which was the rhinoceros which arrived for the carnival of 1751.
> Its journey from Africa via Nuremberg to Venice is perhaps a symbol: something primitive and grotesque coming from that Continent so long thought of as productive of novelties, and being welcomed as 'a change'. There is an element of sadness and futility in the onlookers; the rhinoceros once seen, there remains no more entertainment to be extracted from it, and despite the gesticulating showman his crowd seem already to have exhausted their emotions of wonder and surprise.
> Hogarth (Longhi has been compared to Hogarth) would have wrung something savagely satiric out of such a scene, sympathizing with the beast or with the onlookers. There would have been, in brief, a point to the picture above the mere record-making task of painting what the rhinoceros looked like. Goya (Longhi has been compared to Goya) would have seized like a bird of prey upon the very vacuity of the people he had to depict, enjoying their emptiness as a child enjoys the emptiness of a balloon: he could have blown it out to monstrous swollen proportions. Longhi no doubt had to tread more carefully at Venice, while at the same time his mind had shown neither desire nor ability to express anything other than what it registered as *seen*.
>
> *Levey.*

Across the *portego*, the room on the canal side contains two C18 pictures,
Francesco, Guardi (attr.): *Sala del Ridotto (Gaming Room); Nun's Parlour.*

The passage beyond leads through other rooms to reconstructed rooms of the Tiepolo's country villa. A portico and passageway lead to the Portego del Mondo Novo: a fresco on the ceiling,
Giandomenico Tiepolo: *The Triumph of the Arts.*

and on the largest wall,
Giandomenico Tiepolo: *Minuet at the Villa; Three People Promenading; The New World.*

The frescoes are surprisingly critical of the society they portray. Giandomenico is generally described as 'charming' and 'amusing': this notion is sharply modified by the dwarfs and hunchbacks of the next room—the Room of the Clowns. Fresco on the ceiling,
Giandomenico Tiepolo: *The Swing.*

Frescoes on the walls,
Giandomenico Tiepolo: *Tumblers, Clowns.*

The top floor of the palazzo has china, costumes, a reconstructed chemist's shop and marionette stage of the period.

In the 18th Century, Venice became the City of carnival. Everyone, Doge and beggar alike, paraded in *bauta* and *tabarro*, and in a city once determined to dominate the seas and extend its power and trade into every corner of the globe, there was no longer thought for anything save amusement, perhaps to hide the memory of the faded glory and lost prosperity. But the amusements themselves were so gay, so charming, so tasteful, that pleasure-seekers from all over Europe—gentlemen of leisure, financiers, noblemen and adventurers—flocked to Venice to take part.

One of these visitors was a clever mischief-maker called Ange Goudar, half-satanist, half secret agent, who frequented Venice in order to pick up useful information. He left a thinly-disguised self-portrait in the six volumes of his book *Chinese Spy,* and in 1774 he wrote that 'entering this town, one breathes an atmosphere of voluptuousness that is scarcely conducive to morality. Nothing is to be found there but spectacle, pleasure and frivolous diversions. In other European countries, the madness of carnival lasts but a few days; here it continues for six months of the year'.

174

The carnival opened, in fact, on the first Sunday in October and went on until Lent, with a short interval from Christmas Day till Epiphany. In other words, for six months every year the people abandoned their regular vocations, and, protected by the anonymity of the mask, threw themselves into the lighthearted pastimes which immediately became their main preoccupation. It was a charming, unreal way of life which the Venetians led during these six months when everyone did as they pleased, forgetting age and rank, but in time it grew to seem their only way of life. In other countries and earlier times, the carnival, like the Saturnalia of antiquity, represented a brief moment of licence and indulgence to every whim in defiance of customs and laws, it was, in other words, an orgy, and probably a useful safety valve; after a few days of mad debauch, people would return to their work in a decent and orderly manner.

In Venice, however, the carnival did not have the orgiastic elements which were found elsewhere—and which are still found today in places such as Basle, Cologne and Nice. It has retained an air of elegance and discretion, even in its excesses, and filled one half of the year so pleasantly that the other half was taken up with waiting for it to come round again. Then, as if touched by a magic wand, the town became a kind of fairy world, where all tasks were forgotten, all obligations neglected, and everyone enjoyed himself with unflagging zeal. If a piece of business was absolutely unavoidable, then only the minimum of time was expended on it. A solemn Senator would not wait even to leave the precincts of the Doge's Palace before donning his Pulcinella cloak, pulling its huge sleeves over his ceremonial attire and running down the broad staircase four at a time towards the gondola where a beautiful girl awaited him.

Behind the shelter of the mask, everyone did as he liked, mocking social convention, but remaining nonetheless within the bounds of taste and discretion. These required, for instance, that no-one should ever be recognised, even if his mask did not completely conceal his identity. *'Signora Maschera'* was the correct form of address, admitting no distinction of age or profession.

The mask most usually worn by ladies and gentlemen of rank was an extraordinary white face, adorned with a huge nose shaped like the beak of a bird of prey, through which the wearer breathed. When we come across the mask today in museums or collections of old customs, there seems to be something disconcerting, frightening, almost ghostly about it. For the 18th Century Venetians, however, it had the advantage of covering the face completely. Furthermore, it was always worn with a long black cloak which hid the entire body.

A crowd dressed uniformly in black and masked in chalky

white would have looked doleful and funereal, but fortunately gayer disguises were also to be found in fantastic shapes and gaudy colours. One of the most popular was Pulcinella, who wore a tall white conical hat, a wide tunic, huge trousers, and a colossal nose. This mask had a long history; it existed in Roman times, and it may even have been worn by the Etruscans. Pulcinella is a clown, but a grotesque and sinister clown, strangely bound up with legends of death and sexuality; his tremendous nose is a phallic symbol. Usually Pulcinellas went about in groups, indulging in all kinds of pranks. By tradition they were gluttonous, stuffing themselves whenever possible at other people's expense. They shouted obscene jokes, and, all dressed in white as they were, they seemed like noisy lewd ghosts.

Brion.

The San Barnaba area houses a lot of students and is a good area for cheap eating (see p. 221). The vaporetto can take us back to San Marco.

L'Ambreuil

It is possible to dislike Venice, and to entertain the sentiment in a responsible and intelligent manner. There are travellers who think the place odious, and those who are not of this opinion often find themselves wishing that the others were only more numerous. The sentimental tourist's sole quarrel with his Venice is that he has too many competitors there. He likes to be alone; to be original; to have (to himself, at least) the air of making discoveries. The Venice of today is a vast museum where the little wicket that admits you is perpetually turning and creaking, and you march through the institution with a herd of fellow-gazers. There is nothing left to discover or describe, and originality of attitude is completely impossible.

Henry James.

178

6

Santo Stefano – Rialto – San Cassiano

Leave the Piazza at the bottom end (with your back to S. Marco, at the far left-hand corner) and follow the way until it opens out into a campo. This is the Campo S. Moisè: it has a church (Saint Moses) with a heavy C17 façade. It does not merit a visit, but has one curiosity.

> The Church contains, near the entrance, the grave of Law, the originator of the South Sea Bubble, who died here, 1729. Montesquieu, who met him at Venice, wrote:
> > "C'était le même homme, toujours l'esprit occupé de projets, toujours la tête remplie de calculs et de valeurs numéraires ou représentatives. Il jouait souvent, et assez gros jeu, quoique sa fortune fût fort mince."
> > > *Hare.*

Over the bridge, we enter the Calle Larga Venti Due Marzo: the name celebrates the day in 1848 when the Venetians under Daniel Manin rebelled—unsuccessfully in the end—against the Austrians.

> One of the shops, no. 2251,* is the agent for the Fortuny silks so highly praised by Proust. They are made in a factory of the Giudecca and frequently repeat the patterns of textiles in paintings by Veronese and Tiepolo.
> > *Honour.*

Down the Calle Larga 22 Marzo (note for future reference, on the right, the entrance to Calle delle Veste, which leads to the Fenice Theatre), follow the way to the Ponte delle Ostreghe (oysters): the Bar Ducale and the restaurant Da Raffaele offer a rare opportunity for a drink or meal beside a canal. The way continues into the Campo Santa Maria Zobenigo. Leading off from the far left corner of the campo is the Calle del Dose (Doge) which brings us down to the Grand Canal: the Fondament S. Maurizio gives a good view of Santa

---

* Called Trois.

Maria della Salute (left). To the right of the church you can see the canal façade of the Abbey of S. Gregorio (the inside of which we have seen, p. 81): the C14 doorway, the relief above it, and the trilobate arch windows on either side of it remain from an old abbey.

On the right, the creeper-covered Palazzo Venier dei Leoni; to the left of it, an ochre-coloured building, and then the late C15 Palazzo Dario.

Returning to the campo, we can see ahead the leaning campanile of the church of Santo Stefano. (We come to the church later.) At the far end of the campo is the Church of Santa Maria Zobenigo: the splendid C17 façade is in the full Venetian baroque manner, a display in praise of the founder and his family and unrelated to any religion. On the left is the stump of the campanile (collapsed, 1774). Follow the way, over the Ponte de la Feltrina, and the Ponte de Ca'Zagari, through the Campo S. Maurizio and into the Calle del Piovan. Immediately on the right (number 2762) is a small early C16 building with reliefs.

The way continues to the Ponte S. Maurizio: looking right from the bridge, we can see that the canal goes under the church of Santo Stefano. Over the bridge, we come into the Campo Santo Stefano. There were bullfights here until 1802. In the near corner on your left you will find the Palazzo Pisani (now the Music Conservatory)— begun in the late C16 and completed in the C18. The courtyards are delightfully separated by open *Loggias* on the upper floors.

Out of the Campo, to the right at the far end, into the Campiello S. Stefano, on the right of which is the Church of S. Stefano. The Church has an attractive Gothic doorway (C15); the long nave is flanked by columns of thin ogival arches; the roof is in 'ship's keel' form. A Renaissance-style door at the end of the right aisle leads into the Sacristy:

On the right wall,
Tintoretto: *The Last Supper; Washing of the Feet; Jesus in the Garden.*

The Restaurant outside the Church was formerly a 'Scuola'—a small C15 relief remains on the wall. Follow the way to the top of the Ponte dei Frati: immediately on the right, through the door, is a glimpse of a C17 convent cloister. In the Campo—Campo Sant' Anzolo (Angelo)—on the left, a tiny C12 oratory, recently restored. Behind—the leaning campanile of Santo Stefano. On the right, next to the red-coloured building—a fine C15 pointed-arch façade; on the other side of the Campo, is another C15 pointed-arch façade, and on the left of it a rather severe C17 façade.

The facade of the church of the Madonna dell' Orto (of the garden) is the most intact example of Venetian fifteenth century architecture remaining today. The simple sixteenth century Scuola on the left is attributed to Palladio. The district is poor and neglected, its fine palaces divided into miserable tenements. The church and its neighbouring cloister have been recently restored. From the *Gran Teatro di Venezia*, (but from an earlier source, c 1700).

The Tre Archi bridge, built in 1688 by Andrea Tirali (1660-1737). Like so many similar structures it originally had no walls or balusters. (*Gran Teatro di Venezia*).

The famous bull fights were held in the campo San Geremia until forbidden in 1804. The Palazzo Labia, on the left, in this print from the *Gran Teatro di Venezia*,

was finally completed three decades later and is now the offices of Italian Radio and Television. The church of San Geremia appears in the centre.

Veduta di Canal-Regio al Ponte dei tre Archi.

Veduta di Canal-Regio al Ponte di S. Geremia.

The bridge of Tre Archi over the canal of Cannaregio was restored after the print on page 197 and has been slightly remodelled since. The bridge of San Geremia crosses the same canal near the Palazzo Labia. This pair of engravings was done by Antonio Pietro Zucchi (1726-1795).

Out of the Campo, the way continues down the Calle de la Mandola and over the Ponte de la Cortesia into the Campo Manin, with a Statue of Daniele Manin in the middle. Out of the Campo, on the right, take the Calle de la Vida—it turns left—and an archway on the right leads to a courtyard from which one can see the Spiral Staircase of the Palazzo Contarini del Bovolo (c. 1499).

Turn right on re-entering the Campo, and follow the way, through the Rio Terrà S. Paternian into the Campo San Luca; take the middle left way out of the Campo (the Calle del Forno) and follow the way through the Calle del Teatro to the Campo S. Salvador. The Church is immediately on the right: it is a C16 building, with a mainly C17 façade.

> The interior (reached by a high flight of steps with the ancient crypt beneath) is one of the finest examples of late Renaissance architecture in Venice and forecasting the classical style, with its spaciousness, severity of line and solid yet graceful construction. . . .
>
> *Lorenzetti.*

Third altar on the right,
   Titian: *Annunciation.*
The picture is very dark. It is signed *fecit fecit*—some say to emphasise the miracle of his activity, some say to impress upon his monastic patrons the authenticity of the picture.

On the high Altar,
   Titian: *Transfiguration.*

> It is as impossible to keep untouched by what happens to your neighbours as to have a bright sky over your own house when it is stormy everywhere else. Spain did not directly dominate Venice, but the new fashions of life and thought inaugurated by her nearly universal triumph could not be kept out. It brought home to all Italians, even to the Venetians, the sense of the individual's helplessness before organized power—a sense which, as we have seen, the early Renaissance, with its belief in the omnipotence of the individual, totally lacked. This was not without a decided influence on art. In the last three decades of his long career, Titian did not paint man as if he were as free from care and as fitted to his environment as a lark on an April morning. Rather did he represent man as acting on his environment and suffering from its reactions. He made the faces and figures show clearly what life had done to them.
>
> *Berenson.*

Chapel in the left apse,
    Giovanni Bellini: *Supper at Emmaus.*

Right outside the Church, down the Marzarieta 2. Aprile (on 2nd
April 1849 the Venetians proclaimed resistance to the Austrians
'at all costs'); to the Campo S. Bartolomeo. In the middle of the
Campo there is the Monument to Carlo Goldoni.

> Goldoni—good, gay, sunniest of souls—
> Glassing half Venice in that verse of thine—
> What though it just reflect the shade and shine
> Of common life, nor render, as it rolls,
> Grandeur and gloom? Sufficient for the shoals
> Was Carnival: Parini's depths enshrine
> Secrets unsuited to that opaline
> Surface of things which laughs along thy scrolls.
> There throng the people: how they come and go,
> Lisp the soft language, flaunt the bright garb,—see,—
> On Piazza, Calle, under Portico
> And over Bridge! Dear king of Comedy,
> Be honoured! Thou that did'st love Venice so,
> Venice, and we who love her, all love thee.
>
> *Browning.*

On the right is a house through which a sottoportego passes.

> The house faces the bridge, and its second storey has been built
> in the 13th Century, above a still earlier Byzantine cornice
> remaining, or perhaps introduced from some other ruined
> edifice, in the walls of the first floor. The windows of the second
> storey . . . have capitals constantly varying in the form of the
> flower or leaf introduced between their volutes.
>
> *Ruskin.*

The Salizada to the left leads to the Rialto Bridge. As Hare notes,
the Rialto, which Shakespeare alludes to when Shylock is made to say,

> "Signor Antonio, many a time and oft
> In the Rialto you have rated me
> About my monies"—

refers, of course, to this quarter of the town, and not to the bridge.

> There have been several bridges on this site. The first was a
> bridge of boats. The second was broken during the Tiepolo

revolution in 1310, when the rebels fled across the canal. The third collapsed in 1444 during the Marchioness of Ferrara's wedding procession. The fifth, portrayed in Carpaccio's picture,* had a drawbridge in the middle. It was temporarily removed in 1452 to let the King of Hungary pass by in suitable state with the Duke of Austria; and it became so rickety over the years that one chronicler described it as 'all gnawed, and suspended in the air as if by a miracle'. The sixth was the subject of a famous sixteenth-century architectural competition. Sansovino, Palladio, Scamozzi, Fra Giocondo and even Michelangelo all submitted designs (you may see Michelangelo's, I am told, at the Casa Buonarroti in Florence). Most of the competitors suggested multi-arched bridges, but one, Antonio da Ponte, boldly proposed a single high arch, based upon 12,000 stakes, with a span of more than 90 feet, a height of 24, and a width of 72. This was a daring gesture. Da Ponte was official architect to the Republic, and the Signory was hardly lenient with employees' errors—Sansovino himself was shortly to be imprisoned when his new library building unfortunately fell down. Nevertheless da Ponte's design was accepted, and the bridge was built in two years. It has been a subject of controversy ever since. Many Venetians disliked it at the time, or mocked it as an unreliable white elephant; many others objected when its clean arch was loaded with the present picturesque superstructure of shops; and it has been, until recently, fashionable to decry it as lumpish and unworthy (though several great painters have fondly pictured it, including Turner in a lost canvas).

Structurally, it was a complete success—during rioting in 1797 they even fired cannon from its steps, to dispel the mobs: and for myself, I would not change a stone of it. I love the quaint old figures of St. Mark and St. Theodore, on the station side of the bridge. I love the Annunciation on the other side, angel at one end, Virgin at the other, Holy Ghost serenely aloft in the middle. I love the queer whale-back of the bridge, humped above the markets, and its cramped little shops, facing resolutely inwards. I think one of the great moments of the Grand Canal occurs when you swing round the bend beside the fish market and see the Rialto there before you, precisely as you have imagined it all your life, one of the household images of the world, and one of the few Venetian monuments to possess the quality of geniality.

Morris.

From the left-hand side of the bridge you can see, just over the pontoon of the ferry station a C16 classical-style façade. It is Sansovino's

* Accademia No. 566, Room XX.

Palazzo Dolfin-Manin, now housing the Banca d'Italia. To the right of it, the reddish coloured C15 Palazzo in Venetian Gothic style is the Palazzo Bembo. Hare remarks on the 'beautiful Byzantine cornice above the entresol'. Farther away, on the same side of the Canal, the tallest building is the fine C16 Palazzo Grimani.

From the right side of the bridge you can see, close by on the right, the Fondaco dei Tedeschi, basically an early C15 warehouse for German merchants (and formerly frescoed by Titian and Giorgione) but modified in the last century and restored in this. It is now the General Post Office. On the left is the early C16 Palazzo dei Camerlenghi. The handsome detailing of this Palazzo can be seen at close quarters as we go down the steps.

Over the bridge and along the Ruga dei Oresi we come soon to the entrance (on the right) to the Church of San Giacomo di Rialto: It is an C11 structure and part of the original material remains—see the capitals supporting the vaulted ceiling.

Out of the Church, we go on through the fruit market: the colonnaded buildings are early C16. Take the Porticato of the Banco Giro on the right. (The name comes from the Banco Giro, a circulating credit bank, established here in the C12.) From here, braving the notice, enter the fruit market proper: by the first pillar on the right you find the proclamation stone called Gobbo di Rialto (hunchback of Rialto) from the C16 Statue. The other proclamation stone stands by the façade of S. Marco.

Continue along the Ruga dei Oresi and the Ruga dei Speziali into the Campo de le Becarie. On the right is the Fish Market (built 1907).

> Of all the spectacular food markets in Italy the one near the Rialto in Venice must be the most remarkable. The light of a Venetian dawn in early summer—you must be about at four o'clock in the morning* to see the market coming to life—is so limpid and so still that it makes every separate vegetable and fruit and fish luminous with a life of its own, with unnaturally heightened colours and clear stencilled outlines. Here the cabbages are cobalt blue, the beetroots deep rose, the lettuces clear pure green, sharp as glass. Bunches of gaudy gold marrow-flowers show off the elegance of pink and white marbled bean pods, primrose potatoes, green plums, green peas. The colours of the peaches, cherries and apricots, packed in boxes lined with sugar-bag blue paper matching the blue canvas trousers worn by the men unloading the gondolas, are reflected in the rose-red mullet and the

* I have found this too early.

orange *vongole* and *canestrelle* which have been prised out of their shells and heaped into baskets. In other markets, on other shores, the unfamiliar fishes may be vivid, mysterious, repellent, fascinating, and bright with splendid colour; only in Venice do they look good enough to eat. In Venice even ordinary sole and ugly great skate are striped with delicate lilac lights, the sardines shine like newly-minted silver coins, pink Venetian *scampi* are fat and fresh, infinitely enticing in the early dawn.

The gentle swaying of the laden gondolas, the movements of the market men as they unload, swinging the boxes and baskets ashore, the robust life and rattling noise contrasted with the fragile taffeta colours and the opal sky of Venice—the whole scene is out of some marvellous unheard-of ballet.

Elizabeth David.

Leave the Campo by the bridge (Ponte de le Becarie), under the *sottoportego*, turning left after the next *sottoportego*; take the next *calle* on the right (Calle de l'Erbarol), then left into the Campo San Cassan. The Church (San Cassiano) faces the canal.
In the main Chapel,
Tintoretto: *Crucifixion.*

The Crucifixion is one of the finest Tintorets in Europe. . . . The horizon is so low, that the spectator must fancy himself lying at full length on the grass, or rather among the brambles and luxuriant weeds, of which the foreground is entirely composed. Among these the seamless robe of Christ has fallen at the foot of the Cross; the rambling briars and wild grapes thrown here and there over its folds of rich but pale crimson.

Ruskin.

To leave the Campo we go back behind the Church: then through the Calle del Campaniel to the Grand Canal. We return to the Rialto Bridge and ferry station along the Canal. The Ca'd'Oro is opposite. When you get to the arcaded building fronting the Canal, you will have to go right, between the stalls, to join the Ruga dei Oresi; just before you do so, look across the Canal and a little to the right: you will see a modest palazzo with a portico made up of three rounded arches. The floors above are regarded as highly characteristic of C13 Veneto-Byzantine style.

190

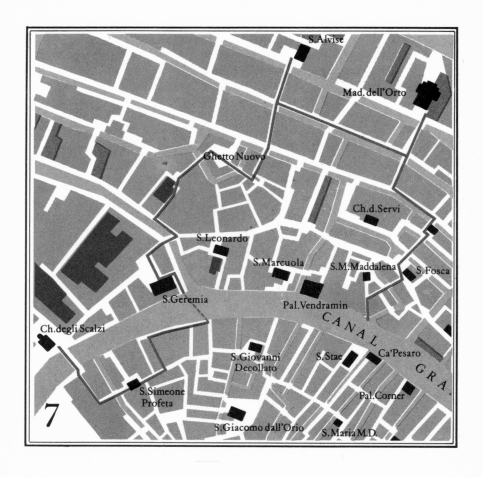

Gobbo: Master, young gentlemen, I pray you, which is the way to master Jew's?

Launcelot: Turn up on your right hand, at the next turning, but at the very next turning of all, on your left; marry, at the very next turning, turn of no hand, but turn down indirectly to the Jew's house.

Gobbo: By God's sonties, 'twill be a hard way to hit.

The Merchant of Venice.

7

San Simeone Profeta – Ghetto – Madonna del' Orto
San Stae

This walk begins at the Railway Station (built 1955), which can be reached by vaporetto. Take the bridge (1934) over the Grand Canal, go straight along the Calle de Ca'Gradenigo (Calle Bergami), go over the Ponte de la Bergama, and in front will be the façade of S. Simeone Profeta. The Church contains a recumbent statue (on a sarcophagus not belonging to it) in the Chapel to the left of the High Altar.

> The face is represented in death, the teeth carefully sculptured beneath; the face full of quietness and majesty, though very ghastly; the hair and beard flowing in luxuriant wreaths, disposed with the most masterly freedom yet severity of design, far down upon the shoulders; the hands crossed upon the body, carefully studied, with the veins and sinews perfectly and easily expressed, yet without any attempt at extreme finish or play of technical skill. This monument bears the date 1317, and its sculptor was justly proud of it; thus recording his name:
> 'Caelavit Marcus opus hoc insigne Romanus,
> Laudibus non parcis est sua digna manus.'
>
> *Ruskin.*

Turn sharp right outside the church, following the wall of the church, under the Sottoportego de la Chiesa into the Salizada de la Chiesa. There, turn left (as directed for Rialto and S. Marco) into Lista Vecchia dei Bari. On the wall on the left an arrow points to the Riva de Biasio: follow it down the Calle del Pugliese; when you reach the Canal, turn right and go past the vaporetto stop to the ferry station.

You can see on the other side of the Canal, almost opposite, the C18 Church of San Geremia; to left of the Church the Palazzo Flangini, its classical detail disposed with characteristic Veneto-Gothic assymetry.

The traghetto brings you to the Fondamenta Ca'Labia. Go through the Church (keeping to the right) into the Campo S. Geremia. On the right is the Palazzo Labia. Ask to see the Tiepolos in the Central Hall.

On the walls,
Tiepolo: *Banquet of Cleopatra;* (Above: *Time Carrying off Beauty*).
Tiepolo: *Embarkation of Cleopatra;* (Above: *Wind Blowing*).

On the ceiling,
Tiepolo: *Poetry on a Winged Pegasus.*

So far as I am concerned, Tiepolo painted largely in vain. I can admire the firm decision of his drawing and his skill in composition, but I can never lose the feeling that his right place is the wall of a restaurant or a theatre curtain. Still, since at the Palazzo Labia we find him decorating a banqueting hall with a secular subject, all is well.

Lucas.

There is no doubt that the famous supper scene, where Cleopatra is shown in the legendary act of dissolving a pearl in a goblet of vinegar, owes something of its inspiration to Veronese's *Supper in the House of Levi*, which is now in the Accademia, even in such small details as the dogs which appear in the right foreground of both compositions.

Masson.

To an earlier age even the subject might have seemed vulgar. But Tiepolo delights in its ostentation and its romantic qualities; there is nothing of high Roman terms in his treatment of it, and little that is specifically Egyptian either. Although the story derives from Pliny, this does not hinder Tiepolo from evolving out of the joint consul with Antony, Plancus, the bizarre oriental figure seated at the left of the table; and in the opposite fresco of *Antony and Cleopatra at the Harbour*, one of the flags gaily bears the German Eagle. The impression rather than exact fact is what matters; ostentation is suggested, not painted literally. The location of Egypt is conveyed by the obelisk and a pair of statues; the attendant soldiers are indicated simply by shafts of halberds rising into the sky; and down the long vista of the scene two lovers confront each other. . . . Whereas the *Banquet* had been the subject of a large picture before it became a fresco, the *Harbour Scene* was virtually Tiepolo's first and final large-scale treatment of the subject. The treatment of it seems rather freer, and possibly it was painted rather later than the *Banquet*. However fast Tiepolo worked, Mengozzi-Colonna (perhaps with assistance) had, on each wall, a considerable task to finish first; and there may well have been some interval for Tiepolo between the two chief scenes. The *Harbour Scene* is conceivably meant to show Cleopatra's landing after her triumphal progress up the river Cydnus, but Tiepolo does not bother to give very precise indications. The lovers advance—Cleopatra in patterned white brocade; their splendid cortege is suggested in small space by massed heads and one single noble horse; and behind them a gang-plank leads to the shell-like prow of a ship. Suggestions of a whole fleet are conveyed by purely theatrical means—brief glimpses of a mast and tackle and the huge sheet of a billowing sail.

The space of sky here seems really wet and windy. The façade frame of the fresco rises nearly to the ceiling, and there at its top astride the clouds the Winds themselves puff their cheeks to fill the sails. *The Banquet* is an immobile and tense scene; but the other wall is all movement, from the lovers who swing out towards the room to the flapping flags and prancing horses who emphasize the restless shifting pageant. . . .

Ignorant but imaginative, Tiepolo placed the scene firmly in sixteenth century Venice, where in fact for him all history took place. . . .

The greatest imaginative painter of the age was really outside the standards his age erected to judge painters. When Cochin said of one of Tiepolo's ceilings that it was 'more beautiful than natural' he indicated, as he thought, its failing. And against this canon of 'Nature' the great artists of the eighteenth century were often to seem culpable and even ridiculous. In England Gainsborough's portraits were to be called 'daubs'; in France Voltaire sneered at Watteau's work and Diderot said he would give *ten* Watteau's for a single Teniers. Tiepolo was, then, exercising his imagination in a chilly climate of critical appraisal. He might be popular with his compatriots, with aristocratic patrons in *retardier* countries; but two of his chief pictorial sources—religion and mythology—were themselves going out of favour. An age of scrutiny, as the eighteenth century supremely was, could hardly be expected to take Tiepolo's work seriously, and the more imaginative he was the more he invited criticism.

Levey.

We leave the Campo at the far right corner, along the Salizada S. Geremia (della Pescaria). After the bridge, left along the Fondamenta de Canaregio. From here you can see the late C17 three-arched bridge (Ponte dei Tre Archi).

Just after the vaporetto stop, there is an archway on the right— to Sottoportego del Ghetto. This will lead you to the Ghetto Vecchio

and the Campo de le Scuole. Facing you is the C17 synagogue attributed to Longhena. Another synagogue is opposite. Out of the Campiello, the Ghetto Vecchio leads into the Ghetto Novo. On the right-hand part of the range on the other side of the Campo is the Jewish museum: the Curator shews the Synagogues.

Jews in Venice were segregated, heavily taxed and subjected to a variety of restrictions. After 1516 they had to live on this island, their houses facing inwards, and the gates locked at night. But, unusually for a Christian state, and they enjoyed the protection of the law. As Shakespeare's Merchant of Venice says

> 'The duke cannot deny the course of law;
> For the commodity that strangers have
> With us in Venice if it be denied,
> Will much impeach the justice of this state;
> Since that the trade and profit of this city
> Consisteth of all nations.'

The community prospered, Italian and German Jews in the New Ghetto, and, later, Levantine Jews in the Old Ghetto. In 1635, the Spanish Synagogue was rebuilt by Loughena. But the taxes outran the profit, and in 1735 the community was officially declared bankrupt.

We leave the Ghetto under the Sottoportego del Ghetto Nuovo. Go over the bridge, then left under the archway (Calle del Ghetto Novissimo), right at the end, under a rectangular arch, immediately left along the Calle dei Ormesini, over the bridge and straight into the Calle de la Malvasia, and over another bridge and straight along the Calle del Capitelo to the Church of S. Alvise. The façade is late C14 Gothic; the interior is a product of C16 re-arrangement and restoration.

On the left on entering and under the singing gallery are eight C15 panels of some charm: (wrongly, it is now thought, attributed to Carpaccio by Ruskin). Looking diagonally across the church we can see three works of Tiepolo. The earliest (1738–40) are on the right wall of the church, just before it narrows to the chancel: *The Flagellation* and the *Crowning with Thorns*. On the right wall immediately in the chancel: *The Road to Calvary*.

> The picture has an hysterical intensity which becomes displeasing, and the scene is too effective to be moving. Tiepolo was almost certainly sincere. But he was not the realist which he tried to be here, with many backward glances not only at sixteenth century Venetian art but also at Rembrandt. The healthy, cheerful people, dignified, well-dressed, of his usual imagining

are pageant-people: what he has produced at S. Alvise are wax-works from the chamber of horrors. The spectacle is degrading, and the trumpets and horses and Roman eagles make a distasteful carnival of the road to Calvary. The three pictures are Tiepolo's most elaborate Passion compositions, and their religious grand-guignol atmosphere makes clear his unsuitability to deal with violent and horrific themes, whatever their source.

Levey.

Tiepolo's energy, his feeling for splendour, his mastery over his craft, place him almost on a level with the great Venetians of the sixteenth century, although he never allows one to forget what he owes to them, particularly to Veronese. The grand scenes he paints differ from those of his predecessor not so much in mere inferiority of workmanship as in a lack of that simplicity and candour which never failed Paolo, no matter how proud the event he might be portraying. Tiepolo's people are haughty, as if they felt that to keep a firm hold on their dignity they could not for a moment relax their faces and figures from a monumental look and bearing. They evidently feel themselves so superior that they are not pleasant to live with, although they carry themselves so well, and are dressed with such splendour, that once in a while it is a great pleasure to look at them. It was Tiepolo's vision of the world that was at fault, and his vision of the world was at fault only because the word itself was at fault. Paolo saw a world touched only by the fashions of the Spanish Court, while Tiepolo lived among people whose very hearts had been vitiated by its measureless haughtiness.

Berenson.

Return over the bridge and along the Calle del Capitelo, and turn left along the Fondamenta beside the canal (the Fondamenta della Sensa). After a while the Gothic façade of the Church of the Madonna dell'Orto appears at the end of a small canal on the left. This is the Ponte de Cá Dabrazzo.

The next turning to the left is the Campo dei Mori. At the opposite corner, facing the canal is one of the delapidated late C13 statues, standing on Roman fragments: this one is popularly called 'Signor Antonio Rioba', a well-known figure in Venetian legend, whose name was used by authors of satires and lampoons. The other end of the Campo leads to the Church.

The façade is the most complete example still in existence of Venetian Gothic of the fifteenth century; it recalls, in its three divisions, the façade of the basilican churches, with its curvilinear profile, central gable and sloping wings. The row of niches, which were the old galleries along the wings, with the *statues of the twelve apostles* . . . are inspired from motives and constitute a characteristic element. The two side windows are Gothic, but of a later period, as also is the doorway (middle XV century) in which newer Renaissance motives contrast with the prevailing Gothic character of the rest of the façade. . . .

Lorenzetti.

On the right side of the nave, just past the 9th Altar, we come to the door into the Chapel, over which is Tintoretto: *Presentation of the Virgin at the Temple.* Two large early works are on the side walls of the Church.

First altar on right
Cima da Conegliano: *St. John the Baptist and Saints.*

Left wall
Tintoretto: *Worship of Golden Calf, Moses Receiving the Tablets of the Law.*

Right wall
Tintoretto: *Last Judgment.*

On either side of the Altar,
Right side
Tintoretto: *Martyrdom of Saint Christopher.*

Left side
Tintoretto: *Apparition of the Cross to Saint Peter.*

Returning down the left wall of the Church we come to a side chapel (marble portraits on the walls), on the altar of which is
Tintoretto: *Saint Agnes Reviving the Roman.*

The last side chapel we reach contains
Giovanni Bellini: *Madonna and Child.*

Back through the Campo dei Mori, over the bridge, through the Calle Larga, and left at the Fondamenta. This is the Fondamenta della Misericordia. There are places for coffee.

Continuing along the Fondamenta della Misericordia, we take the first bridge over the canal to the Campo S. Marziale, and its C17

Church. On the ceiling are paintings by Sebastiano Ricci. In the vault of the chancel,

Ricci: *Holy Father and Angels.*

On the ceiling of the Church
Ricci: *Glory of Saint Martial* (centre).
Ricci: *Arrival of the Image of the Virgin,* and *The Image of the Virgin Carved on a Tree Trunk* (sides).

> He is a disconcerting phenomenon since he began so much, while yet as an artist remaining insipid and usually uninspired. His very attachment to Veronese leads to comparisons in which he emerges eternally the loser. And the existence of Tiepolo, who learnt so much from him, leads to another comparison in which Ricci is defeated again.
>
> But as early as 1705 Ricci was capable of creating the luminous decorative effect of his ceiling in S. Marziale at Venice: an effect considerably enhanced by recent cleaning. To come on this ceiling unexpectedly is to experience something of the excitement it must have generated when it was first shown. It is full of gaily-coloured airborne figures, as in the roundel of the *Arrival of the Virgin's statue,* and has something of the pastel effect of fresco although all the decoration is actually on canvas. Ricci at this time had not settled in Venice, but was still wandering about Italy and the rest of Europe. He had not become quite so obsessed with Veronese as he was to be later, and the S. Marziale ceiling is an unusual example of him creating something for himself, though not without hints from Correggio.
>
> *Levey.*

Out of the Campo over the bridge, down the Calle Zancani, over the next bridge into Campo Santo Fosca. At the other end, a pink palazzo with an overhanging roof is the Palazzo Correr (C15 with C18 modifications), just on the left of which is a narrow calle—the Calle de Ca'Correr: go down this Calle over the bridge (view to right), down the Calle de le Colonete, left at the end along the Calle de Ca'Piovene (Calle del Traghetto) to the traghetto.

If you look across the Canal you will see on the other bank the San Stae vaporetto station with the church behind, on the left a C17 classical building and then a large imposing C17 palazzo—the Palazzo Pesaro, the last work of Longhena. To the right of the ferry station comes first a reddish coloured building (Palazzo Dandolo), then a garden, then a C15 brick palazzo, then a late C16 stone palazzo, and then the elaborate C17 façade and pinnacles of Longhena's Palazzo Belloni–Battagia.

The Campo dei Gesuiti as seen in the *Gran Teatro di Venezia* shows the Jesuit church at the far end of the square on the right before it was completed. The finished facade can be seen in Vissentini's engraving of Canaletto's drawing published in 1754.

Isola di Murano presso a Venezia.

Isola di S. Michele di Murano presso a Venezi.

Islands and Chioggia, an eighteenth century plate most likely by Antonio Piet
Zucchi.

Isola di S. Giorgio Maggiore di Venezia.

Città di Chioggia nel Dogado Veneto.

The singer Bernach, from a cartoon by Zanetti drawn in 1722.

Take the traghetto to the other side. From this side, look back to an C18 building (from which we emerged): to the right of it a small canal (Rio della Maddalena) and then a late C16 palazzo—the Palazzo Barbarigo, with surviving C16 frescoes on the façade. To the left of the ferry station are some examples of Venetian palazzo architecture of different periods: first an C18 palazzo (the lowest of the group), then an early C16 palazzo of a yellow colour, with a finely proportioned Renaissance façade, then a red façade—C15 pointed-arch style (some later alterations), then a yellow-coloured building—an early C18 palazzo, and then—after the garden—the fine early C16 palazzo designed by Coducci—the Palazzo Vendramin. Wagner stayed here and died here in 1883.

At the head of the Campo San Stae is the late Baroque façade of the church of S. Eustachio. Inside, there are several pictures on the walls of the chancel. On the left wall, bottom row, right.

Piazzetta: *St. James Led to Martyrdom.*

> His *St. James Led to Martyrdom*, painted for St. Stae at Venice in 1717, make the work there of the rest of his contemporaries look very slight and artificial—except for that of the young Tiepolo* who was then briskly and misguidedly aping Piazzetta's style. It is true that Piazzetta's drama tends here to Melodrama; but it is significant that he has taken a scene lacking in all supernatural incident, and what he shows in fact is a vigorous old man dragged along in a contorted and confused way by a brawny, tawny, younger man. In character there seems nothing to choose between saint and executioner. Whereas the rococo, however defined, is always aiming to elevate the subject to an exciting operatic movement of grand gestures and radiant personalities, Piazzetta recalls the uncouth literalness of Loth, for example, and seems almost to 'debunk' his subject. Sebastian Ricci's St. Peter Released† from the same St. Stae series, was probably painted a very few years indeed after Piazzetta's picture there, but has obviously nothing in common with it. . . .
>
> *Levey.*

From here you can get back to S. Marco by vaporetto.

* Right wall, bottom row right.
† Left wall, bottom row middle.

206

Excursions

1 Lido

It is true that the beach is ugly and expensive and it is also true that virtually nothing remains of the sandy wilderness known to Goethe and Byron; nevertheless, if you are fond of sea bathing and sun-bathing, go; the sand and the water are pleasant and clean, the bathing facilities are well organised, and the sail across the lagoon (especially the return journey) is delightful.

I like to take the large boat from the Riva degli Schiavoni: it is quick; in the height of the season the sailings are fairly frequent; and the bar is efficient and cheap. Once on the Lido island, it is possible to eat (not cheaply or well) on the way to the beach or on the beach; if you are taking picnic food, do not take fruit—you can buy this from stalls near the beach. (Try the pieces of coconut arranged in tiers under little fountains.)

The Municipal Beach is on the left, when you come to the sea. (Farther to the left—and a long way away—there is a free beach.) The best way is to make up a party of, say, four or six, and hire a hut. The staff at the ticket office are helpful and speak English and will explain the numerous kinds and grades of accommodation available. Information about the bathing establishments along the shore can be obtained from Direzione Attività Balneari, Gran Viale S.M. Elisabetta 2; Tel. 60560.

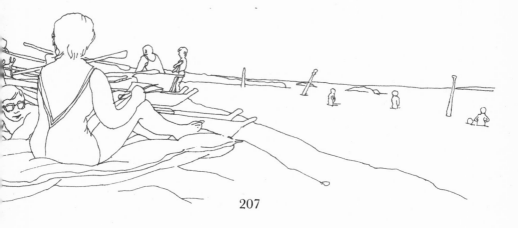

2 Torcello – Burano

The boat leaves from the Fondamenta Nuove. This is not as far as it looks: from the Piazza, under the Clock Tower, right at the Ramo S. Zulian, round behind the Church, straight on over two bridges to Campo S.M. Formosa, out of the far side (by the clock) down the Calle Larga, fourth Calle on the left to S. Zanipolo, and follow the canal beside the hospital to the Fondamenta Nuove.

In the Lagoon we can see the cemetery island, San Michele: we see it at closer quarters from the boat.

> As we go by the Cemetery of S. Michele, Piero the gondolier and Giovanni improve us with a little solemn pleasantry. 'It is a small place', says Piero, 'but there is room enough for all Venice in it'. 'It is true', assents Giovanni, 'and here we poor folks become land-owners at last'.
>
> *Howells.*

> . . . but the dead are only allowed to rest for ten years; then, unless an annual fee is paid, the bones are taken up and thrown, without distinction, into a vast common pit at the end of the island.
>
> *Hare.*

On the way we call at Murano, and set out across the Lagoon. In front and to the right are the Islands of Sant'Erasmo and Le Vignole.

> A most pleasant sunset hour can be spent on the Lagoon, by taking the *Sant'Erasmo* waterbus any late afternoon from Fonda-mente Nuove (No. 13 leaving about 4 p.m.). The church at *Sant'Erasmo* is well worth a visit, being originally a romanesque building: the fine font is Byzantine. There is a good cafe. The return journey during sunset is one of the finest Lagoon experiences one can have. The people on *Vignole* and on *Sant'Erasmo* are welcoming, very hard-working, and ill paid by the middlemen who fetch the vegetables and fruit they grow for Venice Markets.
>
> *Sprigge.*

Before the boat enters the Canal of Mazzorbo, we can see on the right the cypresses of San Francesco del Deserto.

This lonely islet-monastery can be visited directly from Riva Schiavoni or from the Lido on another Torcello waterbus (No. 18) which calls at San Francesco. But in high summer that would be a visit in a crowd. Best of all is a gondola or a sandolo (two oars) from Mazzorbo or Burano, a very pleasant cross-water journey. There is a peacock on the island.

Sprigge.

We stop at Mazzorbo—a quiet spot, with a C14 church, vineyards and a hotel.

La Maddalena, the little inn of Mazzorbo (proprietor Signor Simoncin) good fare, very clean bedrooms, no bath, running water, moderate charges.

Sprigge.

The next stop is Burano. Picturesque fishing village with 'tourist attractions'—notably the Da Romano restaurant and underpaid little girls making lace. Early Tiepolo *Crucifixion* in the Oratory of Santa Barbara, near church.

The next stop is Torcello. (It can be reached directly from the Fondamenta Nuove.)

Seven miles to the north of Venice, the banks of sand, which near the City rise little above low-water mark, attain by degrees a higher level, and hoist themselves at last into fields of salt morass, raised here and there into shapeless mounds, and interrupted by narrow creeks of sea. One of the feeblest of these inlets, after winding for some time among buried fragments of masonry, and knots of sunburnt weeds whitened with webs of fucus, stays itself in an utterly stagnant pool beside a plot of greener grass covered with ground-ivy and violets. On this mound is built a rude brick campanile, of the commonest Lombardic type, which if we ascend towards evening (and there are none to hinder us, the door of its ruinous staircase swinging idly on its hinges), we may command from it one of the most notable scenes in this wide world of ours. Far as the eye can reach, a waste of wild sea-moor, of a lurid ashen-grey; not like our northern moors with their jet-black pools and purple heath, but lifeless, the colour of sackcloth, with the corrupted sea-water soaking through the roots of its acrid weeds, and gleaming hither and thither through its snaky channels. No gathering of fantastic myths, nor coursing of clouds across it; but melancholy clearness of space in the warm sunset, oppressive, reaching to the horizon, of its level gloom. To the very horizon, on the north-east; but to the north and west, there is a blue line of

209

higher land along the border of it, and above this, but farther back, a misty band of mountains touched with snow. To the east, the paleness and roar of the Adriatic, louder at momentary intervals as the surf breaks on the bar of sand; to the south, the widening branches of the calm lagoon, alternately purple and pale green, as they reflect the evening clouds or twilight sky; and almost beneath our feet, on the same field which sustains the tower we gaze from, a group of four buildings, two of them little larger than cottages (though built of stone, and one adorned by a quaint belfry), the third an octagonal chapel, of which we can see but little more than the flat red roof with its rayed tiling, the fourth, a considerable church with nave and aisles, but of which, in like manner, we can see little but the long central ridge and lateral slopes of roof, which the sunlight separates in one glowing mass from the green field beneath and grey moor beyond. There are no living creatures near the buildings, nor any vestige of village or city round about them. They lie like a little company of ships becalmed on a far-away sea.

Then look farther to the south. Beyond the widening branches of the lagoon, and rising out of the bright lake into which they gather, there are a multitude of towers, dark, and scattered among square-set shapes of clustered palaces, a long irregular line fretting the southern sky.

Mother and daughter, you behold them both in their widow-hood—Torcello and Venice.

Thirteen hundred years ago, the grey moorland looked as it does this day, and the purple mountains stood as radiantly in the deep distances of evening; but on the line of the horizon there were strange fires mixed with the light of sunset, and the lament of many human voices mixed with the fretting of the waves on their ridges of sand. The flames rose from the ruins of Altinum; the lament from the multitude of its people, seeking, like Israel of old, a refuge from the sword in the paths of the sea.

The cattle are feeding and resting upon the site of the city that they left; the mower's scythe swept this day at dawn over the chief street of the city that they built, and the swathes of soft grass are now sending up their scent into the night air, the only incense that fills the temple of their ancient worship. Let us go down into that little space of meadow-land.

The inlet which runs nearest to the base of the campanile is not that by which Torcello is commonly approached. Another, somewhat broader and overhung alder copse, winds out of the main channel of the lagoon up to the very edge of the little meadow which was once the plaza of the city, and there, stayed by a few grey stones which present some semblance of a quay, forms its boundary at one extremity. Hardly larger than an English

210

farmyard, and roughly enclosed on each side by broken palings and hedges of honeysuckle and briar the narrow field retires from the water's edge, traversed by a scarcely traceable footpath, for some forty or fifty paces, and then expanding into the form of a small square, with buildings on three sides of it, the fourth being that which opens to the water. Two of these, that on our left, and that in front of us as we approach from the canal, are so small that they might well be taken for out-houses of the farm, though the first is a conventual building, and the other aspires to the title of the 'Palazzo Pubblico', both dating as far back as the beginning of the fourteenth century; the third, the octagonal church of Santa Fosca, is far more ancient than either, yet hardly on a larger scale. Though the pillars of the portico which surrounds it are of pure Greek marble, and their capitals are enriched with delicate sculpture, they, and the arches they sustain, together only raise the roof to the height of a cattle-shed; and the first strong impression which the spectator receives from the whole scene is that whatever sin it may have been which has on this spot been visited with so utter a desolation, it could not at least have been ambition. Nor will this impression be diminished as we approach or enter the larger church, to which the whole group of building is subordinate. It has evidently been built by men in flight and distress, who sought in the hurried erection of their island church such a shelter for their earnest and sorrowful worship as, on the one hand, would not attract the eyes of their enemies by its splendour and yet, on the other, might not awaken too bitter feelings by its contrast with the churches which they had seen destroyed. There is visible every-where a simple and tender effort to recover some of the form of the temples which they had loved, and to do honour to God by that which they were erecting, while distress and humiliation prevented the desire, and prudence precluded the admission, either of luxury of ornament or magnificence of plan. The exterior is absolutely devoid of decoration, with the exception only of the western entrance and the lateral door, of which the former has carved side-posts and architrave, and the latter crosses of rich sculpture; while the mossy stone shutters of the windows, turning on huge rings of stone, which answer the double purpose of stanchions and brackets, cause the whole building rather to resemble a refuge from Alpine storm than the cathedral of a populous city; and internally, the two solemn mosaics of the eastern and western extremities—one representing the Last Judgment, the other the Madonna, her tears falling as her hands are raised to bless—and the noble range of pillars which enclose the space between, terminated by the high throne for the pastor and the semicircular raised seats for the superior clergy, are expressive at once of the deep sorrow and the sacred courage of men who had no home left them upon earth, but who looked for one to come, of men 'persecuted, but not forsaken, cast down but not destroyed'.

Ruskin.

The Town was built by refugees from the Barbarian invasions of Roman Italy, the centre of economic life moved to the Rialto, and the settlements in this part of the Lagoon decayed. The vestiges of the Town are in the centre of the Island. In the season you can have, quite cheaply, a seat in a gondola along the remaining canal. At the end of the canal —Locanda Cipriani, first-class restaurant, prices to match.

The Cathedral, beyond, is mainly C11. Down the sides of the main door, C9 interwoven designs and crosses, C11 grape-vine design.

Inside: the roodscreen is made up of C15 painted panels and early 11th Century marble panels. They are, as Banister Fletcher remarks, one of the typical examples of Byzantine art and shows the close alliance between architecture and subsidiary arts.

Fragments of other panels make up the stair to the Pulpit.

It is supported on a group of four slender shafts; itself of a slightly oval form, extending nearly from one pillar of the nave to the next, so as to give the preacher free room for the action of the entire person which always gives an unaffected impressiveness to the elo-puence of the southern nations. In the centre of its curved front, a small bracket and detached shaft sustain the projection of a narrow marble desk (occupying the place of a cushion in a modern pulpit), which is hollowed out into a shallow curve on the upper surface, leaving a ledge at the bottom of the slab, so that a book laid upon it, or rather into it, settles itself there, opening as if by instinct, but without the least chance of slipping to the side, or in any way moving beneath the preacher's hands. Six balls, or rather almonds, of purple marble veined with white are set round the edge of the pulpit, and form its only decoration. Perfectly graceful, but severe and almost cold in its simplicity, built for permanence and service, so that no single member, no stone of it, could be spared, and yet all are firm and uninjured as when they were first set together, it stands in venerable contrast both with the fantastic pulpits of mediaeval cathedrals and with the rich furniture of those of our modern churches.

Ruskin.

In the apse are mosaics: twelve apostles (C12, but much restored) in Ravenna style; Virgin, C13. On the opposite wall, in mosaic, the *Universal Judgement.*

In the left-side chapel, on the floor, an early C14 tomb. Beside the main door, a font, supported on a piece of column.

This history of Torcello has for its background in the 4th and 5th Centuries the savagery and slaughter of the Migration period. Like a late reminder of this a font of barbarian vigour stands on a column, half-forgotten, in the gloomiest corner of the church. Here we have a Lombard or Friuli craftsman and for once can sense the under-tone of non-classical violence over which the order of Mediterranean culture only triumphed after heavy fighting.

Decker.

3 Gondolla Ride (with Gesuiti church)

Travellers may often complain of the weariness of the Venetian sights, and of their being too much like one another. It is quite true that they are so, but let those who are bored sit still in their gondolas.

Hare.

If you can afford a gondola ride, on no account miss it. Possible rides are endless; the only rule is to agree the duration and price with the gondolier before you start. A tariff is displayed on the boat.

Here is an hour-ride which I have found particularly attractive at about four in the afternoon.

From the Piazza, take the Mercerie (under the Clock Tower) down to Campo San Bartolemo; continue through the Campo and on past the Post Office: the first bridge crosses the Rio del Fontego dei Tedeschi. Take the gondola from here, go out into the Grand Canal and up the Rio dei Santi Apostoli to the Church of the Gesuiti. Leave the gondola to see the showy C18 interior and

First Altar in left transept
Tintoretto: *Assumption* (in very poor state).

Altar on left, nearest entrance
Titian: *Martyrdom of Saint Lawrence* (light switch behind column on right).

Titian's art underwent somewhat of a change about 1540. The problems posed by mannerism are reflected in his work and shake his serene vision of the world. He wrenches his forms, foreshortens his figures and underscores his lighting by a dramatic

214

use of chiaroscuro, particularly in the *Martyrdom of Saint Lawrence* (1557). There are relatively few important Titians remaining in Venice. It is unfortunate that this striking painting has been allowed to darken considerably and remain in bad condition.

Chastel.

In this virtuoso night piece, the beam from heaven, the torches and the glowing fire beneath St. Lawrence's grille, illuminate the pagan idol, flicker on the marble temple and glint on the soldiers' helmets. One is even inclined to suspect that the painting is an excuse for the pyrotechnic effects and the use of dark, rich colour rather than an attempt to render the Saint's agony. Apart from a fresco by Raphael in the Vatican, it is the first successful nocturne in the history of art. Like the *Assumption* in the Frari, it anticipates the baroque style. It therefore exerted considerable influence when night-pieces became so popular throughout Europe in the seventeenth century.

Honour.

Back in the gondola, continue out to the Fondamenta Nuove, then down the Rio dei Mendicanti; after S. Zanipolo, turn right along the Rio S. Marina and right up the Rio della Panada, fork left along the Rio San Canciano, and turn left along the Rio dei Miracoli—along the side of the Miracoli church. After a crossing of four canals, we reach the Rio del Fontego dei Tedeschi again.

4 *Ridotto*

Dr. Zamarchi is the occupier of a flat beside the Ponte dei Barretteri (No. 4939). It is the Ridotto della Procuratoressa Venier—a small elegant gaming house of the C18, which has remained virtually intact, with stucco, paintings, and carved mantelpieces, cupboards and doors of the period. Ask for permission to visit (Tel. 28594); take flowers.

An attractive route from the Piazza is: under the clock, down the Marzaria de l'Orologio; right along the Ramo San Zulian into the Campo S. Zulian; keeping to the left of the church, through the Campiello S. Zulian, still keeping left; then, sharp left under the Sottoportego Primo Lucatello and the Sottoportego Secondo Lucatello.

Gambling played quite as large a part as the theatre in the lives of 18th Century Venetians. They were so passionately addicted

215

to it, it is said, that they would gamble the clothes off their back. At sunrise, it was not unusual to meet a man slinking home in the dawn, having lost everything save the cloak which hid his nakedness.

Everywhere in the City people gambled, and particularly in the public establishments known as *ridotti,* where a tradition of complete discretion (helped, of course, by the mask during carnival time) allowed the most distinguished members of the aristocracy to mingle freely with the crowds of ordinary citizens, adventurers and swindlers who naturally swarmed in the card-rooms. These houses were luxuriously decorated with multi-coloured stucco and sumptuous ormolu and were frequented by pretty women of easy virtue who came to seek clients, by *entre-metteuses,* spies, and ruined scions of noble families, all rubbing shoulders with the professional gamblers. One could embark on many a delightful adventure in the *ridotti,* without ever losing sight of the faro bank, where fortunes were being swallowed up, or the *basetto* table, where the more impecunious gamblers trembled as they risked their last sequin. This multiplicity of gaming rooms in a city where by tradition games of chance were forbidden, seemed to keen observers a most revealing sign of the times. In fact, all the time the Venetians were engaged to the full in the dangers and excitements of war, conquest, exploration, foreign trade, the taste for gambling having been effaced by these momentous events. As the Political activity of the Serenissima declined, however, cards and dice gradually replaced the oar and the sword.

Brion.

Appendices

1 Staying and Eating in Venice

Staying:

Of the posh hotels, the Danieli (p. 109) and the Gritti are undoubtedly the best known. A currently fashionable hotel in this category is the Cipriani: it is on the Guidecca island, facing away from the Piazzetta, but connected with the Molo by a private motor-launch service. An hotel a little less expensive is the Luna (Calle Vallaresso)—it is comfortable and efficient in a rather characterless way.

At a more modest level, the Accademia (a few minutes from the gallery) attracts the more studious visitor; the Fenice (near the theatre) has a true Aspern Papers atmosphere and attracts a theatrical clientele.

At the bottom end of the scale there is a cluster of hotels near the station—in and off the Lista di Spagna. The Albergo Gallini (Calle della Verona, San Marco) is well spoken of. The Hotel Rialto (by the bridge) is cheap and 'authentic': it requires demi-pension, but the restaurant is also good value; it has rooms facing the Canal—which is attractive but noisy.

For very cheap rooms for men only—the Casa dello Studente (July—September).

Eating:

Anyone who wants a really cheap meal can go out to a bakery which has its own pizza oven and buy a large slice of pizza for a few lire, repair to the nearest bottiglieria or wine shop, and there drink a litre of wine and eat his pizza for little more than a shilling. . . .

Elizabeth David.

You can easily and cheaply assemble a picnic lunch out of bread, cheeses, olives and ham, with fresh fruit and a bottle of wine, or you can eat very cheaply at the University Mensa near Campo San Barnaba. This student area has a number of cheap

restaurants: leading out of the Campo is the Calle Longa, with da Bruno on the left, and under the Sattoportico dei Nobili the Fondamenta del Squero, with da Oreste on the right. Beyond da Oreste the Sottoportico Calle de le Romite leads to the slightly more expensive Locanda Montin (with garden).

There is a group of fixed price restaurants in the moderately cheap class in the Lista di Spagna and a small group in the Calle delle Rasse between the two wings of the Danieli. In the very cheap class, Frommer recommends alla Branza and da Nino al Teson in the Campiello de la Pescaria (beyond the Danieli, over three bridges and left down the Calle de la Pescaria). For a modestly priced meal in an agreeable spot, there is the Ristorante da Raffaele (p. 179).

Serious cooking costs, of course, very much more, but this perhaps is the moment to stress that Italian cooking at its best is very much more distinguished than is commonly believed: it is seasonal and highly regional and almost as expensive as the French equivalent.

Elizabeth David has collected some traditional Venetian recipes and gives other Venetian recipes based on chefs' recipes from restaurants in Venice. This is her list. They are generally obtainable at restaurants described below, but each restaurant serves other local dishes and has its own specialities.

HORS D'OEUVRE

Pasta in brodo	Pasta in broth
Crostin	Fried bread with cheese and anchovies
Vitello Tonnato	Veal with tunny fish sauce

RISOTTO

Risotto in Capro Roman	Mutton Risotto
Risotto de Secole	Veal Risotto
Risotto de Scampi	Scampi Risotto
Risotto di Peoci	Mussel Risotto

FISH

Zuppa di Peoci	Cooked Mussels
Grancevole	Crabs
Molecche	Soft Shell Crabs
Scampi alla Griglia	Grilled Scampi
Triglie alla Veneziana	Red Mullet in Wine
Sogiole alla Veneziana	Sole with Wine Sauce
Coda di Rospo	Rospo Fish Tail
Pesce San Pietro	John Dory
Baccalá Mantecato	Creamed Salt Cod

Fegato alla Veneziana   Fried Liver and Onion
Carciofi alla Veneziana   Venetian Artichokes

Restaurants:

MADONNA: Calle della Madonna (over Rialto bridge and turn left). Bright bustling taverna, with good unsophisticated food.

POSTE VECIE: Beside the fish market (p. 189). Similar food, more intimate atmosphere.

PAGANELLI: Campo San Zaccaria (off Riva degli Schiavoni). The food here can be very good indeed: it is served in rather austere surroundings and is, therefore, relatively cheap.

    Particularly to be recommended are the risotto di peoci and the filetto di San Pietro al vino bianco. The risotto takes time to prepare; it is best to order it half an hour before you arrive (Tel. 24–324).

LA COLOMBA: (off the Frezzeria). Very good food, well served under a canopy in an attractive courtyard (a little hard to find). They produce a recipe book of their special dishes.

ANTICO MARTINI: (near Fenice Theatre). Elizabeth David's Filetto Casanova originates here (though here they put the popular Worcester Sauce in with the marsala). Other specialities are:

Cocktail di Crostacei   Sea Food Cocktail
Tagliolini al Prosciutto   Noodles with Ham from San
  S. Daniele   Daniele
Filetti di Sogliola Martini   Fillet of Sole 'Martini'
Rognone alla Fiamma   Calf kidneys Flambé
Dolce della Casa   House Cake

2 *Table of Events*

C5–C7   **Barbarian invasions of Roman Empire. Torcello and other islands settled by refugees from mainland.**
697   **First Doge.**
811–827   **Seat of Government moved to Rialto (Rivo Alto).**

829	Remains of St. Mark brought from Alexandria (p. 35).
C9–C11	Growth of sea trade and naval power.
1044	San Marco consecrated.
1177	Pope Alexander III and Emperor Frederick Barbarossa reconciled (p. 36).
1203	Armies of IVth Crusade take Constantinople: Venice acquires large territories in Near East and immense quantities of plunder.
C13–C14	Long struggle with Genoa, rival maritime power; Venetian victory at Chioggia 1380.
1310	Unsuccessful rebellion of Bajamonte Tiepolo (p. 123).
1355	Unsuccessful bid for power by Doge Marin Faliero (p. 59).
1453	Constantinople falls to Turks.
Late C15	Loss of several eastern colonies to Turks; defeat of navy at Sapienza (1441) beginning of three centuries of gradual decline.
1498	Vasco da Gama sails round Africa.
C16	Austrian-Spanish Hapsburgs expand on mainland, Turks in east. Loss of Morea (Peleponnese) and Cyprus (fate of Marcantonio Bragadin—p. 131).
1606	Climax of long quarrel with Rome, Venice excommunicated.
C17	Continued struggle with Turks. Loss of Crete. Short-lived reconquest of Peleponnese.
C18	Foreign defeats, shrinking trade, social atrophy; carnivals and masquerades.
1797	Surrender to Napoleon, who passed town to Austria.
1805	Ten years under Napoleonic French rule.
1815–68	Austrian colony; era of particular oppression and poverty.
1868	Joined to Italy.

3 Special Interests

(i) Museums, Galleries and Permanent Exhibitions

1. Accademia	Pictures
2. Scuola di San Giorgio	Pictures by Carpaccio
3. Hellenic Institute	Icons

4. Ca'd'Oro	Furniture, Persian Carpets
5. Palazzo Rezzonico	C18 pictures and furnishings
6. Sansovino Library	Bindings—Byzantine, Venetian and Foreign, C10–C18 Codexes— Byzantine, Venetian and Italian
7. Zecca (Marciana Library)	Codexes (Greek and Latin). Books, Manu- scripts, Incunabulae
8. S. Marco Treasury	Byzantine goldsmith work, Icons, Bindings, Byzantine and Oriental objects (mainly ecclesiastical)
9. San Marco: Marciano Museum	Flemish Tapestries, Persian Carpets
10. Doge's Palace	Armoury
11. Arsenal	Naval Museum
12. Casa Goldoni (see under 'Courtyards')	Theatrical Library
13. Scuola di S. Giovanni Evangelista	Architectural fragments sculpture
15. Palazzo Querini— Stampalia	Library, pictures, C18 and Early C19 furniture
16. Archaeological Museum (the entrance is under the Sansovino Library)	
17. Patriarchal Seminary	Pictures, sculpture, Lapidary collection
18. Correr Museum	Venetian Art and History collection, including (apart from the fine picture gallery) docu- ments, robes, coins, seals, naval souvenirs and arms, and the Museum of the Risorgimento (illust- rating the history of Venice from the fall of the Republic to 1945)
19. Fondaco dei Turchi (to S. Marcoula vaporetto station, then across the Canal by traghetto)	Natural History

20. Palazzo Venier dei Leoni	Guggenheim Collection —C20 pictures
21. Palazzo Pisani (Campo S. Stefano)	Musical Instruments
22. Murano Glass Museum (to Murano island—by boat from the Fondamenta Nuove)	Glass
23. Museum of Burano Lace (to Burano island—by boat from the Fondamenta Nuove)	Lace
24. Lagoon Museum (To Torcello, by boat from Fondamenta Nuove)	Fragments found at Torcello

(ii) *Courtyards*

1. No. 6359. Calle della Testa (in front of SS. Giovanni e Paolo, p. 128, take the Ponte del Cavallo; the *Calle* is on the right).
2. No. 2793. Calle dei Nomboli—'Casa Goldoni'— (From the vaporetto station of S. Tomà, take Calle del Traghetto until it opens out into a small square on the right. Through the square turn left along the Fondamenta S. Tomà, and go over the Ponte S. Tomà).
3. S. Giorgio dei Greci—Churchyard with C15 wellhead (p. 114).
4. Ca'd'Oro (p. 145).
5. Palazzo Contarini del Bovolo (p. 185).
6. Larger and more formal courtyards will be found in the Doge's Palace (p. 50), Palazzo Pisani (p. 180).

(iii) *Cloisters*

1. Dell'Abbazia (p. 80).
2. Cypress Cloister and Bay Tree Cloister—Cini Foundation (p. 61).
3. S. Francesco della Vigna (p. 115).
4. S.M. del Carmine—entrance from Sacristy (p. 168).

(iv) *Gardens*

1. **Palazzo Venier dei Leoni (housing Guggenheim Collection) (p. 81)**	Leafy, with statuary. Open Mon. Wed. Fri. 3–5 p.m.
2. **Eden Garden (Guidecca Island: by boat to the Redentore, the garden lies along the nearby canal, the Ramo Campiello al Rio della Croce)**	Laid out with flowers and lawns. Belongs to Princess Aspasia of Greece.
3. **Patriarchial Seminary (Vaporetto stop Salute)**	
4. **Palazzo Grassi (Vaporetto stop S. Samuele)**	C18 garden, now with open-air theatre for events of the Centre of Arts and Costume.
5. **Cini Foundation, S. Giorgio (p. 61)**	

(v) *Theatres*

An evening at the Fenice is imperative. The entrance halls were remodelled in 1957, but the interior, after being burnt in 1836, was remade as it was when it was first built in 1792 (p. 179).

Of the theatres of the days of the Republic several have been demolished—one (the *Rossini*) gave its name to a cinema. There remain the *Goldoni* (along Calle del Lovo from Campo S. Salvatore) and *San Moisè* (off the Calle Larga XXII Marzo) both closed. There is a modern open-air theatre at the Palazzo Grassi and the *Teatro Verde* at the Cini Foundation on S. Giorgio. The Institute of Theatre Studies in the Casa Goldoni houses a library and memorials of the life and times of the C18 Venetian writer Goldoni.

(vi) *Villas of the Veneto*

The 'Malcontenta', the Villa Pisani at Stra and other villas can be visited by motor launch (apply CIT, Piazza S. Marco). These and others can easily be reached by car. There are car-hire offices near the Piazzale Roma.

4 Table of Artists

Elsewhere in Italy	Venice	Elsewhere in Europe
Giotto	Paolo Veneziano c. 1290–1358	
Donatello	Jacopo Bellini 1400–1470	Van Dyke
Piero della Francesca	Antonio Vivarini c. 1415–c. 1484	
Mantegna	Gentile Bellini 1429–1507	Memling
Verrocchio	Giovanni Bellini 1430–1516	
	Bartolemo Vivarini c. 1432–c. 1499	
Perugino	Alvise Vivarini c. 1446–c. 1505	
	Andrea da Murano?–1502	
	Coducci c. 1440–1504	
Leonardo	Cima da Conegliano 1459–1518	
	Carpaccio c. 1465–1525	Dürer
	Giorgione c. 1478–1510	Holbein
	Palma the Elder 1480–1528	
Michel-angelo	Lotto 1480–1556	
	Sansovino 1486–1570	
	Titian c. 1488–1576	El Greco
	Basaiti c. 1500–	
	Paris Bordone 1500–1571	
	Palladio 1508–1580	Rubens
	Tintoretto 1518–1594	
	Aless. Vittoria 1524–1608	
	Veronese 1530–1588	Van Dyke
	Palma the Younger 1544–1628	
A. Carraci	Longhena 1568–1662	
Giordano	Bombelli 1635–1716	Heinz
Claude	Amigoni 1675–1752	
	Piazzetta 1682–1754	Watteau
	G. B. Tiepolo 1696–1770	Hogarth
	Canaletto 1697–1768	Wilson
	Longhi 1702–1785	Goya
	Guardi 1712–1793	
	Bellotto 1720–1780	
	Giandomenico Tiepolo 1727–1804	
	Canova 1757–1822	

5 Short Bibliography

Berenson, B.	The Venetian Painters of the Renaissance, 1894	G. P. Putnams' Sons
do.	On Lotto, 1895	do.
Berger, J.	Permanent Red, 1960	Methuen & Co, Ltd.
Brion, M.	Venice, The Masque of Italy, 1962	Elek Books Ltd.
Burckhardt, J.	The Civilisation of the Renaissance in Italy, translated S. G. C. Middlemore, 3rd Ed.	Phaidon Press Ltd.
Chastel, A.	Venice Observed (notes on the plates)	Zwemmer
David, E.	Italian Food, 1954	Macdonald & Co. Ltd. (Penguin Books Ltd. 1963)
Decker, H.	Venice, 1957	Thames & Hudson Ltd.
Demus, O.	A Renaissance of Early Christian Art in 17th Century Venice	University Press, Princeton
do.	Late Classical & Mediaeval Studies in honour of Albert Matthias Friend, Jr. (Ed. K. Weitsman, 1955)	do.
Fletcher, Banister	A Short History of Architecture	Athlone Press
Goethe, J. W.	Italian Journey, translated Rev. A. J. W. Morrison and Charles Nisbet	Collins, Sons' & Co. Ltd.
Gombrich, E. H.	The Story of Art	Phaidon Press Ltd.
Gould, C.	An Introduction to Italian Renaissance Painting, 1957	Phaidon Press Ltd.
Hare, A.J.C. and St. Clair Baddeley	Venice, 6th Ed. 1904	George Allen & Unwin Ltd.

Honour, H.	The Companion Guide Venice, 1965	Collins, Sons' & Co, Ltd.
Levey, M.	Painting in XVIII Century Venice, 1959	Phaidon Press Ltd.
Lorenzetti, G.	Venice and its Lagoons, translated J. Guthrie, 1961	Instituto Poli-grafico dello Stato
Lucas, E. V.	A Wanderer in Venice, 8th Ed., 1914	Methuen & Co, Ltd.
Masson, G.	Itallian Villas & Palaces, 1959	Thames & Hudson Ltd.
Morris, J.	Venice, 1960	Faber & Faber Ltd.
Pevsner, N.	An Outline of European Architecture, 5th Ed., 1961	Penguin Books Ltd.
Pignatti, T.	The Venice of Carpaccio, 1958	Skira
Ruskin, J.	The Stones of Venice, 2nd Ed.	George Allen & Unwin Ltd.
do.	Modern Painters, 2nd Ed. 1892	do.
Sprigge, S.	The Lagoon of Venice, 1961	Parrish
Tumiati, P.	Canute-Like lay the Lagoon, 1969	Financial Times
Wittkower, R.	Art and Architecture in Italy, 1600/1750, 1958	Penguin Books Ltd.

Index

231

232

233